A Catalogue of the Compositions of
FREDERICK DELIUS

Frederick Delius by Sir William Rothenstein

A Catalogue of the Compositions of

Frederick Delius

Sources and References

ROBERT THRELFALL

Delius Trust : London 1977

CONTENTS

LIST OF ILLUSTRATIONS

Except where otherwise stated, illustrations are of MSS in Delius's own hand

It was brought home to me . . . how much more one learns about a man's work by handling . . . it with the intention of writing about it than one does by simply enjoying it.
  (Sir John Rothenstein, *Brave Day: Hideous Night*, London, 1966).

Who shall say that there is no romance in musicology?
  (Edmund H. Fellowes, *Memoirs of an amateur musician*, London, 1946).

INTRODUCTION

It was that great Englishman, Dr. Samuel Johnson, who defined a lexicographer as 'a writer of dictionaries; a harmless drudge, that busies himself in tracing the original . . .' Another great Englishman, Sir Thomas Beecham, opined that a musicologist was a man who could read music but could not hear it. Caught between the definitions proposed by these two savants, then, who should the compiler of such a book as this one be; why would he undertake it; and whom could he expect to read it?

The compositions of Frederick Delius, perhaps because of their singular and transcendent beauty, have not yet been thoroughly subjected to the clear-sighted scrutiny needed to list them in detail in all their bibliographical confusion. Just as the late Maurice J. E. Brown was understandably reluctant to apply reference numbers and letters to Chopin's series of matchless piano poems, to encode the works of the author of *In a Summer Garden* with quasi-algebraic formulae may seem little short of blasphemy. However, though no-one would consider Köchel's massive volume a substitute for the works of Mozart, yet 'K' is far more than a mere tool of musicology: just as every performer understands the importance of exactly-calculated pitches, durations and speeds, an attempt at listing equally accurate detailed information regarding the composition and publication of a composer's entire *oeuvre* may likewise play its part. One might perhaps echo the student in W. H. Auden's tale: '. . . that is a matter of opinion. The number of pages is a matter of fact'.

In the particular case of Frederick Delius—who still awaits his complete and definitive biographer—any attempt to stem further proliferation of error, whether biographical or bibliographical, must be particularly welcome. Born as he was in the house opposite—as was Dvořák (though for a different reason . . .); celebrating his 60th birthday on his 61st; buried in 1934 and again (and in another country) in 1935; the story in which these were but three landmarks evidently included enough sufficiently unusual material to excite the interest of any serious biographer. It is a far cry from the sensitive dreamer all-too-firmly fixed in the public's imagination, the pathetic invalid of too many familiar portraits, to the vigorous man at the height of his fame and his career in, say 1908: travelling on the night train from the première (in Liverpool) of *Brigg Fair* to London, for a performance there next day of the still rarely-heard *Life's Dance*; attempting, however unsuccessfully in the event, the rôle of conductor of his own major scores; embroiled in the deliberations of the equally ill-fated Musical League; moving quickly from the Bal des Quatz' Arts in Paris (*what lovely women were there* he wrote to Bantock on 20 May 1908) to the première in Munich of his greatest work (*My 'Mass' made an enormous impression—in fact far more than I ever expected*, ibid. 9 June 1908); and thinking of taking up painting the female nude whilst leaving the writing of music to Ernest Newman, *as he knows so much about it* (ibid. 16 June 1908). This was the man in such physical condition, 'lean, wiry and strenuous in every movement' (John F. Runciman) and so full of energy that Beecham, himself no weakling in any way, had difficulty in keeping up with him on their joint Norwegian trip that very year. This was the man 'with a heart like a lion . . . of whom Nietzsche would have said "Here is one of the great despisers"' (Eric Fenby). Ruthless in discarding any musical ideas he considered of lesser worth, and as thrifty in preserving for later use those that passed his critical judgment as he was frugal in saving manuscript paper that had only been used on one side, he combined the skill and the imagination which inform all true works of great art. Not only was he creator of some of the most poetic tone-pictures and dramatic choral works 'in the language', but he was equally a dedicated craftsman, who polished even a comparatively slight chorus written for a competition festival until he was completely satisfied with it, and gave lifelong concern to the minutiae of the multilingual translations of his songs, in which painstaking attention to details of declamation mark the mature examples. Study of the revisions and differing versions which result from his quest for perfection calls for as complete and accurate listing as possible of the source-material, then, for its starting point.

SCOPE AND PLAN OF THIS WORK
The aim of the present volume, therefore, is simply stated: to list all of Delius's compositions, in all their editions and versions, published or unpublished, in such a way as to render the resulting corpus of information immediately accessible to the user of the book. I am not presumptuous enough to think there are no gaps or mistakes in my work—though admittedly it is always easier to spot, and even to correct, the errors of others than those of oneself: may my errors, however, be mine own, and not mere copies of another's! I have endeavoured to examine personally every MS, publication and edition described, or photographs thereof, except in those few cases to which attention is especially drawn. Missing works and MSS are another thing; some it seems may not break surface until the sea gives up its dead. But life is short: time presses: better the present imperfect work than none at all; and in drawing attention now to such gaps in the present state of our knowledge as they arise, I hope it may be possible to issue any additional information if and when it comes to hand.

The absence of opus numbers to Delius's works throws one back on to other methods of classification: alphabetic would be useless; purely chronological could be misleading (in view of the many overlaps of great works with small). Hence my decision first to divide the music systematically into categories, then to observe chronological sequence within each category as far as possible; the various divisions being as follows:

1 Dramatic works
2 Works for voices and orchestra
3 Works for solo voice and orchestra
4 Works for unaccompanied voices
5 Songs with pianoforte accompaniment

6 Works for orchestra alone
7 Works for solo instrument(s) and orchestra
8 Chamber music
9 Pianoforte solos
10 Appendix: arrangements, notebooks etc.

In conclusion, a schematic chronological conspectus of the principal works, followed by a detailed alphabetical index of all names and titles in all the languages concerned, should enable each work or movement to be traced and set in its context with the minimum of difficulty. Each entry gives information under the following headings as appropriate:

Title and style of work: in translation also, if authentic.

Date: with supporting evidence if necessary. Delius usually dated his MSS with the original date of composition, which thus often found its way to the printed copies. These dates take primacy in my listings, with any secondary sources from contemporary writings, letters etc. in confirmation or amplification as necessary. If Delius is occasionally inconsistent, who are we to blame him?

Dedication: in the actual words used.

Key: if appropriate.

Compass: of solo songs.

Details of instrumental forces called for. Orchestrations are given in the usual abbreviated form; instruments bracketted do not call for separate players.

MSS: the various MSS traced are listed, cross-referenced to Rachel Lowe's *Catalogue* (v. inf.) where appropriate, or briefly described.

Publications: dates, plate nos., and any additional information, e.g. revisions or corrections, are given.

Performance: date and place of first, and first British, performances; details of some other early performances also included in some cases.

Arrangements: details of MSS, publications etc.

Source of words used in vocal settings; details of translation, if appropriate; basis of story of operas.

Notes: references to the standard primary source-books on Delius; quotations from articles or letters which refer to the work in question; matters of general interest; brief notes (in case of vocal settings) on a few other composers' uses of the same words or poets, with no pretence to completeness (Delius's *ipsissima verba* are always italicized and his characteristic spelling and punctuation are respected).

I give no durations of works: average lengths appear in publishers' catalogues, but actual performances vary widely; even Beecham was known to add a minute or two to a short number like the *Walk to the Paradise Garden*, whilst some versions of the *First Cuckoo* are on record lasting a mere half the time taken by others . . . In general, I have not attempted any detailed bibliography; less still have I touched on a discography. Both of these subjects deserve, and are receiving, the attention of specialists in their respective fields. Likewise, thematic incipits are not used for several good reasons: the consequent delay, extra bulk and cost of this book would have been prohibitive; the necessity is not so great for the works of a composer such as Delius as for one of the classics who may well have written dozens of symphonies, concertos or sonatas in the same few keys, and a mere two-stave 'index of first lines' seems more misleading than useful in this context. Alas, those stern critics who bemoan the absence of incipits in such a book as this are sometimes the first to denounce them as an extravagance when they are used!

SOURCES CONSULTED

Primarily, the chief source utilized is the complete MS and printed legacy of Delius the composer. As many different copies as possible of the printed editions, and all MSS accessible (or photographs thereof) have been inspected; the principal variants being noted as appropriate.

As regards the extensive MS holding of the Delius Trust, London, this has already been catalogued and described in detail by Rachel Lowe in her 'Catalogue of the Music Archive of the Delius Trust' (London, Delius Trust/Boosey & Hawkes, 1974). My indebtedness to this primary source-book is evidenced by the frequency with which its author's initials recur through my own pages, as also by the absence of any duplication of her work called for by my own.

Recently an agreement has been reached under which those MSS of Delius compositions hitherto in the archives of the publishers Boosey & Hawkes are being transferred to the Delius Trust Archive. This is already being implemented, although some time may elapse before all detail of assimilation into their new home is completed: hence my listing still shows these items under their previous ownership. Unfortunately, it has proved impossible so far to locate the MSS formerly held by Winthrop Rogers & Co., which firm merged with Hawkes & Co. in the 1920s, the latter in turn joining with Boosey & Co. to become Boosey & Hawkes in 1930.

Some early original MSS, e.g. those of the well-known *Seven Songs from the Norwegian* and the three *Shelley Songs*, now appear to be lost. More serious lacunae are the MSS of all those works originally published by Verlag Harmonie of Berlin and by F. E. C. Leuckart originally of Leipzig, as also of the two popular pieces for small orchestra first published by Tischer & Jagenberg: their very existence after two world wars may indeed be considered doubtful. Covering as they do many, nay, most, of the composer's mature works, their loss is to be specially deplored in view of the light they might throw on pre-publication alteration, etc.; it may be presumed, however, by analogy with later cases, that the first editions represent a fairly faithful copy of the *Stichvorlagen* in their final state. Copies of all other MSS that it has been possible to trace, with the exception of those believed still to remain in the Beecham library, are now held in the Delius Trust Archive, in most cases on microfilm.

The following earlier typescript listings of MSS have also been consulted:
(i) 'List of musical MSS and scores set aside by Mr. Fenby . . .'
(ii) 'Second list of MSS and musical scores & libretto.'
(iii) 'Contents of Trunk and Tin Box . . . received this 4th day of June 1952 . . . for and on behalf of Sir Thomas Beecham.'
(iv) 'List of Delius works in Sir Thomas Beecham's study.'

The first two of these schedules were drawn up by Eric Fenby shortly after Jelka Delius's death in 1935; the third records the transfer of MSS to Sir Thomas Beecham at the time of work on his biography of the composer, while the fourth establishes the subsequent Delius material in the Beecham library. After Beecham's death in 1961, the bulk of these MSS returned to the Trust—trunk, tin box and all; with the exception of certain MSS, principally some of those claimed by Beecham in a declaration he made in 1947 as having been presented to him 'for his sole use and as his sole property' by the composer in 1929. These latter works, and a few other MSS not transferred back to the Trust in 1961, are believed to remain in the Beecham Library. Sir Thomas, despite his sardonic views on musicologists, would not have refused to have his possessions duly listed in detail; unfortunately, since his death it has so far been impossible to obtain the necessary particulars from his estate; hence my descriptions of some of the items in question may appear somewhat truncated.

Where possible, I have endeavoured to identify the copyists of any non-autograph MSS mentioned. Easy in the cases of well-known or distinctive hands such as those of Florent Schmitt or Peter Warlock (Philip Heseltine), it proved hardly more difficult to name certain recent and well-known professional copyists. Identification of the scribe responsible for many MSS of Delius's works from the late 1890s however has so far met with no more success than efforts to name the author of the second part of the Book of Isaiah: hence I refer perforce to this still unknown hand as that of 'the Paris copyist'.

Some of the old or original printed editions of Delius's music exhibit frequent inaccuracies of notes, clefs, accidentals etc. In some cases, e.g. that of *A Mass of Life*, these are probably the results of the full scores being printed before they had stood the test of public performance; in others—principally the works published just after the first War by Augeners—the position was further exacerbated by the incompetence (or absence) of 'professional' proof reading at the very time when Delius's increasing physical afflictions were forcing him to rely more and more on the assistance of others.

In a letter to Beecham dated 10 March 1929, Delius writes: *I wish* you, *who so thoro'ly understand my music and who are the one authority as to how it should be played—would re-edit my music as you are planning. Nothing would please me better*. In an endeavour to set this state of affairs into motion, a brave beginning was made by the Delius Trust in 1951 in launching a Collected Edition—the first to be undertaken for any contemporary British composer—of the 'Complete Works, revised and edited by Sir Thos. Beecham'. Rightly starting with those works hitherto 'lithographed' (i.e. *Appalachia, Sea Drift* and the Piano Concerto—but not, alas, although proposed, *A Mass of Life*), engraved scores were produced incorporating Beecham's detailed editing of dynamics and 'hairpins', tempi and some corrections. *Brigg Fair* followed (in an American edition only); *Florida*, in hand at the time of the great conductor's death, appeared shortly afterwards as an 'op. posth.' Universal Edition next followed suit with a long-overdue engraved score of *Paris* (hitherto also only 'lithographed'); this likewise incorporated much of Beecham's editing (though unattributed in this particular case). The corrected and edited scores of *North Country Sketches* and *Eventyr*, likewise promised in this series at the time of Beecham's death, never materialized in that form. Recently, however, scores of these and the other 'Augener' orchestral works have been reprinted by Stainer & Bell, incorporating many corrections but without Beecham's editing. Most of the chamber music and all the songs have also now been reissued with largely corrected musical texts. Meanwhile, a more-or-less complete set of printed scores in the original editions, bearing Beecham's markings, is deposited in the Delius Trust Archive.

As most of the published works are now out of copyright in the USA, more American arrangements or reissues may exist than I have been able to trace; any further information from America on these lines would be particularly welcome, and will be gratefully acknowledged.

ACKNOWLEDGMENTS
Now in conclusion comes the most pleasant duty of all, when due thanks must be rendered to those whose help is here recorded.

First, it will be immediately evident that the production of this book in its present form would have been impossible without the unanimous support of the Delius Trust, London. No reference to that body can fail first to mention the late co-Trustee, Dr. Philip Emanuel, to whose great kindness and interest I am particularly indebted. The encouragement of his successor, Major Norman K. Millar; the wise counsel of Sir Thomas Armstrong; the enthusiasm of Mr. Felix Aprahamian; all these are to be chronicled, as also is the help of the various officers of Barclays Bank Trust Company Ltd., who one and all have shown that so large an establishment is indeed no 'faceless monster' when it comes to day-by-day affairs. The Herculean labours of the Trust's present Archivist, Dr. Lionel Carley, in preparing for publication and where necessary translating the vast surviving correspondence to and from the Deliuses, are still in progress; but he has never begrudged me his time, his knowledge, or reference to his library, in answering my queries or assisting me to locate material. I have already spoken of the Catalogue of the Trust's music archive written by his predecessor, Rachel Lowe; I must now add my personal thanks for her continuous interest and encouragement, and for much stimulating discussion and correspondence over the years.

Turning to others whose valuable assistance is most gratefully acknowledged, first mention must be of Eric Fenby. His work with the stricken composer is itself enough to ensure him fame second only to Delius's own; his generosity in amplifying his written recollections again and again, and submitting to my persistent questioning with charm, humour and enthusiasm is to be recorded with deep appreciation. Two members of the Delius Society, London, also deserve special mention in this context: Stephen Lloyd's diligent search for dates and details of performances has been and is being conducted with exemplary thoroughness; his kindness in putting his results to date at my disposal has ensured more accuracy in this area than I could ever have achieved otherwise, and a number of important corrections to previous records have been thus established. Likewise, Christopher Redwood's long-standing interest in all matters Delian, and his present position as editor of the Delius Society's Journal, have made him a 'clearing house' for much unusual information; and I must thank him for sharing this with me, as also for many lively and informative talks.

All those I have named so far have personal or other connections with the 'Delius Industry', but many more have been hardly less helpful. Oliver Neighbour, Music Librarian, Reference Division, The British Library, London, and Edward N. Waters, Chief of the Reference Department, Music Division, The Library of Congress, Washington DC, USA, have made research in those two National collections a great pleasure. Many members of the staff of Messrs. Boosey & Hawkes Music Publishers Ltd. have helped me in various ways over the years; and of these, if I only name Martin V. Hall, director, and J. Malcolm Smith, librarian, it is because their patience with me has been the most remarkable. May I assure the many other friends and correspondents, both here and abroad, whose help in various ways has been timely, that their encouragement is much appreciated, even if I do not mention them all by name.

Thanks for permission to reproduce extracts from copyright musical material are hereby extended to the following publishers:

BOOSEY & HAWKES MUSIC PUBLISHERS LTD:
> Avant que tu ne t'en ailles
> Fennimore and Gerda
> Piano Concerto
> A Village Romeo and Juliet

OXFORD UNIVERSITY PRESS LTD. (Music Dept.):
> Song: Venevil
> Piano Prelude no. 1

STAINER & BELL LTD:
> String Quartet

UNIVERSAL EDITION:
> In a Summer Garden

All other plates of musical illustrations, and all quotations from letters, are copyright by the Delius Trust, London, and are quoted here with their permission.

The portrait drawing of Delius by the late Sir William Rothenstein is reproduced by permission of the artist's executors, Sir John Rothenstein and Mr. Michael Rothenstein; I am also grateful to Sir John Rothenstein for permission to reproduce a quotation from his own autobiographical volume, *Brave Day: Hideous Night*.

May the information here gathered together be a useful source of reference to all who share an interest in Delius's music and are working to further its appreciation. In conclusion, may I once again request all who use or refer to this book to share with the Delius Trust and myself whatever additional knowledge of these matters they may have or obtain. Such further information, corrections and all extra data will be welcomed by the compiler, c/o Barclays Bank Trust Co. Ltd., Central London Area Office, Juxon House, 94 St. Paul's Churchyard, London EC4M 8EH, and gratefully acknowledged. It would be hoped to publish all such addenda and corrigenda in one of the regular musical journals in due course.

ROBERT THRELFALL,
London, Christmas 1976.

REFERENCES AND ABBREVIATIONS

TB Sir Thomas Beecham, Bart: *Frederick Delius*, Hutchinson, (London 1959).

GC Eric Fenby: *Delius* (The Great Composers series), Faber and Faber (London 1971).

LKC Lionel Carley: *Delius: The Paris Years*, Triad Press (London 1975).

MC Sir Thomas Beecham, Bart: *A Mingled Chime*, Hutchinson (London 1944).

Chop Max Chop: *Frederick Delius*, Verlag Harmonie (Berlin 1907).

CD Clare Delius: *FD: Memories of my Brother*, Ivor Nicholson & Watson (London 1935).

EF Eric Fenby: *Delius as I knew him*, Bell (London 1936).

Gray Cecil Gray: *Peter Warlock: a memoir of Philip Heseltine*, Jonathan Cape (London 1934).

Holland A. K. Holland: *The Songs of Delius*, Oxford University Press, (London 1951).

BL British Library, London.

RL Rachel Lowe: *A Catalogue of the Music Archive of the Delius Trust*, Delius Trust/Boosey & Hawkes (London 1974).

MM Alan Jefferson: *Delius* (Master Musicians series), Dent (London 1972).

SM 7 Robert Threlfall: 'Delius Music MSS in Australia', in *Studies in Music* (Perth, W.A., Vol. 7, 1973).

Nettel Reginald Nettel: *Music in the Five Towns, 1840–1914*, Oxford University Press (London 1944).

DLP Lionel Carley and Robert Threlfall: *Delius, a Life in Pictures*, Oxford University Press (London 1977).

DT Delius Trust Archive, London.

PW Peter Warlock (Philip Heseltine): *Frederick Delius*, John Lane the Bodley Head (London, first edition 1923; second edition, enlarged, 1952. References to the second edition are given in parentheses).
Note: all dates quoted from PW are from this work; but in his earlier article in the *Musical Times*, (London, March 1915, pp. 137–142) he had given a number of slightly differing dates for both works and events.

1935/1 'List of musical MSS and scores set aside by Mr. Fenby'.

1935/2 'Second list of MSS and musical scores & libretto'.

1952 list 'Contents of Trunk and Tin Box ...'

Beecham Libr. list 'List of Delius works in Sir Thomas Beecham's study'.

} see above p. 12

Note also:

I. A. Copley: 'Warlock and Delius—a Catalogue', in *Music and Letters* (London, vol. 49 no. 3, July 1968).

Christopher Redwood (ed.): *A Delius Companion*, John Calder (London 1976).

Robert Threlfall: 'Delius in Eric Fenby's MSS', in *Composer* (London, no. 57, Spring 1976).

Fred Tomlinson: *Warlock and Delius*, Thames Publishing (London 1976).

Der hügel wo wir wandeln liegt im schatten,
Indes der drüben noch im lichte webt . . .

Plate 1: Zanoni. Page 3 of draft MS

I Dramatic works:

I/1 ZANONI
[Draft of incidental music for a dramatised version of Edward Bulwer Lytton's romance *Zanoni* of 1842].

Date: *Aug 3/88*, according to Beecham Libr. list. (The first leaf now missing). FD to Grieg, n.d. [late summer 1888, St. Malo]: *I have dramatized . . . Zanoni . . . & write incidental music for it, as an opera it doesn't go well.*

Scenes: Act I [Prelude and] Scene 1 [Book the Second, Chapter 1]
Scene 2 [do., Chapter 10]
Scene 3 *Pastorale* [do., Chapter 4]
End of Act I [do., Chapter 5]
Act II *Prelude* Scene 1 [Book the Third, Chapter 4]
Scene 2 [do., Chapters 8, 13]
Act III
Act IV

MS: Autograph draft piano score DT 39 ff 3–13 (RL 134–5), pp. 3–21, incomplete. (Cue lines are given, from the chapters indicated).

Publication: none. Facsimile of pp. 8–9, RL 136–7. Facsimile of p. 3, *see Plate 1.*

Notes: Not in PW. TB 49, where it is stated that 'only a portion of the prelude and opening scene remain'. LKC 17. See RL 134–5 for full description.
The music headed *Pastorale*, Act I scene 3 above, was used as the basis of the Silver Stream music in *Irmelin*, Act II, bars 684 sqq. The following short passage was also transferred to *Irmelin*, Act III, bars 494–503.
For dramatic links with *The Magic Fountain*, see entry below for that work.

Another similar project was mentioned in letters to Grieg the following year: FD to Grieg, n.d. [1889] . . . *I write zwischenactsmusik for "Emperor and Galilean"*; and later: *I have sketched out something from "Emperor and Galilean"*. Henrik Ibsen's drama of this title dates from 1873. See TB 49, 52. References by Beecham (TB 52) to 'Tiberius' and 'Cleopatra' as further possible subjects for dramatic works are apparently based solely on mentions by Sinding, in letters to FD during October 1889, that he is sending the books of these titles 'by Stahr' that FD had evidently requested; these projects are hence best discounted.
More concrete, if fragmentary, evidence surrounds another such proposal, however. An undated letter from FD at Croissy (where he lived from October 1889 until 1891) to Emma Klingenfeld, one of Ibsen's German translators (to whom FD was referred by the playwright himself) mentions . . . *mein Vorhaben 'Das Fest auf Solhaug' als ein Lyrisches Drama zu bearbeiten*. A drafted setting of a 4-part choral song to words from Act II, scene 8 of this work—but in the original

Norwegian ('Herude, herude skal gildet stå')—survives in DT 36 ff 10–11, see p. 84 inf. There are also sketches headed 'Solhaug' and 'Fest auf Solhaug' in Notebook III, see Appendix. Incidental music to this play in Emma Klingenfeld's Ger. trans. (including this same chorus—'Es locket ins Freie') was commissioned from Hugo Wolf and written in 1890–1 (see Frank Walker, *Hugo Wolf*, London, 1951 edition, pp. 279–282 and 476). A little later, Emma Klingenfeld made the Ger. trans. of Delius's own opera, *The Magic Fountain*, v. inf. p. 24).

I/2 **IRMELIN**
Opera in three Acts—(published score)
[Lyric Drama (v. Runciman, inf.)]
Libretto [from a text] by the Composer.

Date: 1890–2 (PW); these dates are accepted by TB 56–8 and, with
reservations, by LKC 27, 30–1.
John F. Runciman (Musical Courier, 18 March 1903, pp. 16–17, reprinted
in *A Delius Companion* pp. 13–18) gave 'finished in 1891'; in any case
composition of the bulk of the music probably dates from the latter part
of the period stated (some is known to have been sketched or written
earlier, v. inf.).

Characters: Irmelin, a Princess *Soprano*
The King, her Father *Bass*
Nils, a Prince, having lost his way, Swineherd of Rolf *Tenor*
Rolf, a Robber *Bass-Baritone*
Old Knight *Baritone*
Young Knight *Tenor*
Warlike Knight *Bass*
A Maid *Mezzo-Soprano*
The Voice in the Air *Soprano*
Chorus of Robbers, Knights, Guests, Women, Wood-Nymphs, Girls and
Boys. [up to 8-part]

Scenes: Act I   Scenes 1–6   Irmelin's room in the Royal Castle
       Act II   Scene 1   A swamp in the forest
               Scene 2   A hall in Rolf's stronghold [Sc. 2, 3, 4 in MS]
               Scene 3   In the mountains [Sc. 5 in MS]
       Act III   Scene 1   A hall of the Royal Castle
               Prelude
               and Scene 2   Outside the Royal Castle
[*Note:* the Prelude in Act III bears no relation at all to the orchestral
'Irmelin Prelude' q.v. p. 158].

Orchestra: 3 (& picc). 2. CA. 2. BsCl. 3—4. 2. 2 Cornets. 3. 1—Timp. Cym.
Trgl. Glockenspiel—Harp—Strings.
On the stage: Acts 1 & 3: Horns (in the distance)
               Act 3: Pipe

MS: (*a*). Autograph full score, 3 volumes, Beecham library; also MS
orchestral material. [I have been unable to consult these MSS].

(*b*). Vocal score by Florent Schmitt [n.d. but 1893–4], Boosey & Hawkes
archives, pp. 275, bound. (FD to Jutta Bell, 29 May 1894: *I am working
with a friend all day at a reduction of my opera for piano and voice*).
This score has no titlepage. The piano arrangement is chiefly in
Schmitt's hand, but FD sometimes drew the brace and clefs for the
piano staves. Some of the piano part appears to be in FD's hand,
e.g. part of the 'Silver Stream' music in Act II, and in Act III the latter
part of scene 1 and much of scene 2. The voice parts, words (in Engl.) and
stage directions are all in FD's hand. Ger. words are added in pencil,
in an unidentified hand.

(*c*). Vocal score by Dennis Arundell (?1952–3). Prepared for Sir Thomas Beecham's use, for the first performance and publication. Original MS not traced, but photographic copies DT 42 (RL 153) and Boosey & Hawkes archives, pp. 227, bound, Eng. only. In the hand (presumably) of Dennis Arundell, this score differs in its piano arrangement from Florent Schmitt's earlier one: through the inclusion of more orchestral detail, it is consequently less pianistic at times.

Note: it appears that bars 960–976 of Act III as published were a later interpolation, for they do not appear in the early MS (b) above.

Publication: 1953, Boosey & Hawkes 17365, *Vocal score* by Dennis Arundell, Eng., pp. 170. (An errata sheet to music, also incorporating some alterations to the original words, was issued with this vocal score). *Libretto*, Eng., pp. 38, separately published at the same time (this agrees in most cases with the alterations established by the above errata sheet). *Full score* unpublished.

1955, Boosey & Hawkes 17799. 'Concert Suite from Act II. Edited and arranged by Sir Thomas Beecham'. ['Scenes from Irmelin'], full score, pp. 70. No material issued or available: Sir Thomas used the MS parts of Act II of the opera, suitably marked and 'sewn up', for his own performances of this suite.

Note: The suite comprises the following bars from Act II of the opera, the voice parts being either omitted or cued in as necessary: 1–40, 55–74, 80–91, 264–314, 485–496, 543–9, 554–592, 618–657, 680–778, 803–835; the whole being played in a continuous unbroken sequence.

Performance: 4, 5, 6, 7 (matinée) & 9 May, 1953, Oxford, New Theatre. Edna Graham (Irmelin), Thomas Round (Nils), George Hancock (Rolf), Oxford University Opera Club Chorus (cond. J. A. Westrup), Royal Philharmonic Orch. cond. Sir Thomas Beecham; producer: Dennis Arundell (who also conducted the matinée on May 7).
22 November 1953, broadcast;
6 December 1954, televised;
(parts of Acts II–III only; with Joan Stuart and Thomas Round, Royal Phil. Orch. cond. Beecham).

Story: according to Beecham, v.inf., the plot 'unites two stories of different origin . . . The legend of Irmelin, a king's daughter who rejects the marriage offers of a hundred noble suitors, is Northern and early mediaeval. That of the Princess and the Swineherd belongs to the less dateable period of the Fairy-tale.'

Notes: TB 56–8; also Sir Thomas Beecham, 'An unknown opera of Delius's youth', *Daily Telegraph & Morning Post*, Saturday 21 March 1953 (Reprinted in *A Delius Companion*, pp. 71–3).
Some sketches for the music are to be found in Notebook III, see Appendix. Also, portions of the music used for the 'Silver Stream' episode in Act II, bars 684 sqq. and for the meeting of Nils and Irmelin in Act III, bars 494–503, are taken from the music earlier sketched for *Zanoni* (RL 135, plates 33–4), v. supra.

A four-note motif becoming increasingly prominent in the later stages of the work (e.g. Act III bar 393) is later to be found playing a fundamental part in both *Songs of Sunset* and *Cynara*.

During the period of work on this first completed opera, other subjects had been reviewed and other librettists contacted before Delius finally decided, or was forced, to write his own words. LKC 30 quotes a letter from Richard Le Gallienne to his mother dated 27 February 1892, in which he says: 'We have sketched out the plot of a little opera together on the story of Endymion . . .'

I/3 **THE MAGIC FOUNTAIN**
Der Wunderborn—La source enchantée
Lyric Drama in three Acts
Text and Music by FD.

Date: 1893 (PW, on evidence of vocal score, v. inf.), 1894–5 (TB 65–6)
Runciman (see ref. under *Irmelin*) gives date 'finished in 1894'; FD's
correspondence with Mrs. Jutta Bell during 1894 dates work on the
libretto as still in progress.

Characters: Solano, a Spanish Nobleman *Tenor*
Watawa, a young Indian girl *Soprano*
Wapanacki, an Indian chief *Bass*
Talum Hadjo, a seer *Bass*
A Spanish sailor *Bass*
Chorus of Sailors, Indian warriors, Indian women, Night-Mists and
Invisible Spirits of the Fountain.

Scenes: Act I   Scene 1 On board ship
                     Scene 2 On the coast of Florida
            Act II   Scene 1 Indian village in the forest
                     [Transformation scene to the Everglades]
                     Scene 2 Talum Hadjo's abode
                     Scene 3 The Everglades
            Act III   The Everglades
The action takes place in the sixteenth century.

Orchestra: Picc. 3. 3. CA. 3. BsCl. 3. Sarrusophone in C—4. 3. 3 (Tenors).
1—Tymp. Cym. Tamt. Bs. Dr. Trgl. Glockenspiel—Harps 1–2—Strings.
In the autograph MS full score, the woodwind instruments appear in an
unusual order partly resembling the practice of the mature Wagner, viz:
Flutes, Clarinets, 'Hautboys', Cor Anglais, Bassoons, Bass Clarinet,
Sarrusophone.

MS: (*a*). Fragment of early draft of scenario, DT 39 f 50 (RL 139–40).

(*b*). Autograph full score, DT 6 (RL 37–40), pp. 74, 64, 88; Eng. only.
(MS orchestral material, BBC Library).

(*c*). Vocal score by Florent Schmitt, Boosey & Hawkes archives; card
covers reading 'The Magic Fountain/Opera in three acts by Frederick
Delius/Piano score by Florent Schmitt' (Jelka Delius's hand). Titlepage
in French and German (the latter, very neat, in red ink). Ger. trans. by
Emma Klingenfeld. Date added on titlepage: 1893. Not consecutively
paginated.
Almost all the music, voice parts included, is in Florent Schmitt's hand
(an obvious exception, in FD's own hand, is the last page of the prelude
to Act III, perhaps a later insertion). The Eng. words and stage directions
are in Delius's own hand; the French ditto, in mauve ink, are probably
in Schmitt's; the Ger. ditto, in red, are in a hand so far unidentified. This
piano arrangement calls for 4 hands during the storm interlude in Act I,
also for the dance at the climax of Act II.
Loosely inserted in this score is a sheet of foolscap on which Philip
Heseltine has commenced a transcription of the libretto and summary of
the plot. It breaks off in the middle of Act II.

(*d*). Vocal score by Eric Fenby, prepared for Sir Thos. Beecham in 1953
with a view to publication and performance, DT 7 (RL 40), pp. 192,
Eng. only, entirely in the hand of Eric Fenby. *See plate 2.*
Note: this vocal score by Eric Fenby comprises a different piano
arrangement from that by Florent Schmitt.

Publication: none. Facsimile of p. 5 of full score of Act I in Catalogue of
Exhibition 'Delius and America', London Borough of Camden, 1972.
Ditto, RL plate 9, p. 38. Facsimile of a page of Florent Schmitt's vocal
score of Act I, DLP 29.

Performance: Under consideration for Prague 1895–6 and Weimar 1896,
see RL 39, but no performance eventuated. Performance contemplated
by Sir Thomas Beecham in 1953, but abandoned.
A studio performance for later transmission by the BBC, 30 July 1977;
Katherine Pring (Watawa), John Mitchinson (Solano), Richard Angas
(Talum Hadjo), Norman Welsby (Wapanacki), BBC Concert Orchestra,
cond. Norman Del Mar.

Story: The basis of the story is the discovery of Florida in 1513 by Ponce de
León, and the legends then current of the Fountain of Perpetual Youth.
See RL 37, 139–140.
Although Delius exchanged a considerable correspondence with his
friend and one-time neighbour (at Solana Grove), Mrs. Jutta Bell, on
details concerning the writing of the libretto, the work as it now stands—
for better or for worse—is apparently entirely his own, with the possible
exception of Watawa's soliloquy which opens Act 3.

Notes: TB 65–70, 72–3; RL 37–40, 139–40; Robert Threlfall, 'Delius's
unknown opera: The Magic Fountain,' to appear in *Studies in Music*
(Perth, W.A., Vol. 11, 1977).
For details of cross references between this work and other compositions
by FD, see RL 39 where links back to *Florida* and on to *Koanga* and
even *Sea Drift* are noted. See also TB 38, 66, 99 (though the 'hundred
bars' mentioned by him as transferred from the prelude of Act II to form
the prelude to Act III of *Koanga* is on the generous side: only 47 bars
being in fact used). In addition, some other links have been noted by PW
148–9 (130): he draws attention to one with *A Mass of Life*, and he
indicated a resemblance between the principal theme of *Life's Dance* and
a motif in Act I of the opera in his (MS) piano arrangement of the
former work. Further, in Acts II and III of the opera, a motif found in
the earlier (and unfinished) *Légendes (Sagen)* for piano and orchestra is
extensively used to represent Talum Hadjo's warning, *see plates 2–3*.

The underlying dramatic motif, that of the fatal nature of the Fountain
of Eternal Life to one unprepared to partake thereof, is also found in the
book *Zanoni*, cf. Zanoni's warnings to Glyndon, Bk. III Chap. 4, 14;
Mejnour's warnings, Bk. IV Chap. 3, 7.

Philip Heseltine, writing in the *Musical Times*, March 1915, p. 138,
states: '. . . the libretto—written in rhymed verse by the composer
himself—shows markedly the influence of "Tristan", whereas the music
is conceived on wholly non-Wagnerian lines'. Despite this opinion, the
score of *The Magic Fountain* is richer in use of leitmotiven than any other
Delius score, early or late (see study by the present author listed above).

Plate 2: The Magic Fountain. Vocal score by Eric Fenby, p. 116

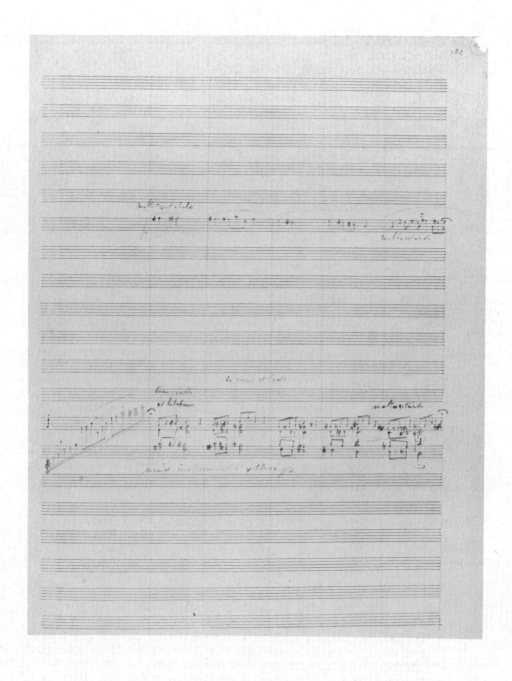

Plate 3: Légendes (Sagen) for piano and orchestra. Page 22 of pencil draft score

I/4 KOANGA

A lyric Drama
Opera in three Acts with Prologue and Epilogue
[Original] Text by C. F. Keary (and see below, Libretti)
('in its outline the story of this musical drama has been taken from George
W. Cable's tale of *The Grandissimes*'—according to programme of first
performance of excerpts in 1899).

Date: 1895–7 (determined from FD–Jutta Bell correspondence; RL 141).

Characters: Don José Martinez, a planter *Bass*
   Simon Perez, Don José's overseer *Tenor*
   Koanga, an African prince and Voodoo priest *Baritone*
   Rangwan, a Voodoo priest *Bass*
   Palmyra, a mulatto ['quadroon' in MS and later edition] half sister
   to Clotilda *Soprano*
   Clotilda, wife to Don José Martinez *Contralto*
   Negro slaves, Creole dancers, Servants

   In the Prologue and Epilogue:
   Uncle Joe, an old slave *Bass*
   Planters' daughters:
      Renée, Hélène, Jeanne, Marie *Sopranos*
      Aurore, Hortense, Olive, Paulette *Contraltos*

Scenes: Prologue: The Verandah of an old and stately Plantation House
   Act I   The Plantation of Don José Martinez
   Act II   The front Verandah of Don José Martinez' house with
            garden
   Act III The swamps—
            The Plantation of Don José Martinez
   Epilogue: The same as the Prologue, at dawn

The action takes place on a plantation on the Mississippi in Louisiana.
Time: the second half of the eighteenth century.

Orchestra: 3 (incl. Picc). 2. CA. 3. BsCl. 3. Contra—4. 3. 3 (Tenors). 1—
   Timp. Trgl. BsDr. Side Dr. Tenor Dr. Tamtam. Tambourine. Tomtom.
   Glockenspiel—2 Harps—Strings.

   Offstage: Cowhorn (Act 1)
   On the stage: 2 Banjos (Act 2)

MS: (*a*). Autograph full score, 3 volumes, Jacksonville University,
   Florida, USA (formerly DT, who now retain a microfilm and
   photoprints). Lacking titlepage, pp. 73, 86, 166 (but v. infra), n.d. Eng.
   text, with Ger. trans. (?in Jelka Delius's hand) interlined or patched over.
   The following modifications have been made in this score:
   Act I. Four pages, the first headed 'Einlage zum I. Akt' and containing
   the orchestral introduction, precede the numbered pages of the act; the
   original p. 17 appears to be missing.
   Act II. A 14-page 'I. Einlage im II. Akt' follows p. 31, and a 3-page
   'II Einlage im 2. Akt' follows p. 66; the original pp. 24–29 are missing.
   Act III. A new introduction (derived from that to Act II of *The Magic
   Fountain*), pp. 1–7, replaces the deleted (but not removed) pp. 1–10. The
   original pp. 44–5 are missing, and a deleted page follows p. 58.

(*b*). Full score, 3 volumes, copy in the hand of Eric Fenby (n.d. but 1930, v. EF 96), Boosey & Hawkes archives, pp. 69, 71, 117. Eng. words only, apparently pencilled in at first (? from original score); then differently inked in, partly in Fenby's hand, partly in another's, to agree with the revised libretto as used for the first publication, v. inf. At the point in Act II where Palmyra's aria begins, Jelka Delius has pencilled: 'This is an aria composed for the Elberfeld performance. There are no English words. I put a litteral [sic] translation on top. Jelka Delius'.

This score was at first reconstructed from the parts, the autograph score being then mislaid, but in the later stages it was copied from the rediscovered autograph, v. EF 96.

(*c*.) Vocal score by Florent Schmitt, Boosey & Hawkes archives, n.d., pp. 58, 84, 67. The piano part, in mauve ink, is in Schmitt's hand, FD's own hand being in evidence in the voice parts and Eng. words of Act I. The words are in Eng., with Ger. below (in red ink) in Acts I–II; Act III being in Ger. only, with Eng. added over the staves, in part.

In this MS there is no prelude to Act I, and the original prelude only to Act III; the two 'Einlagen' in Act II being laid in in sheets, in FD's hand, with Ger. words only.

(*d*). Vocal score, copy of (*c*) above, principally in the hand of the 'Paris copyist', DT 46 (RL 157–8), oblong paper, bound, pp. 90, 81, 88, Eng. and Ger. words, the latter in red ink. The Eng. stage directions are in FD's own hand, as also are various alterations and some insertions, including Palmyra's central aria in Act II. The original prelude to Act III appears, marked 'wegzulassen'; there is no prelude to Act I.

(*e*). Vocal score, another copy of (*c*) above, in the hands of several different copyists, 3 volumes, card-covered, Boosey & Hawkes archives, pp. 93, 72, [73]. This score, interleaved with plain sheets and headed 'Szenische Einrichtung von J. Goldberg', was prepared for Jacques Goldberg, the producer of the opera at its first performance, v. inf. Ger. words only, in different hands in each act (partly in 'Schrift').

In this MS, Palmyra's aria is included in the main text of Act II, but there are no preludes to Acts I and III. A note states '14 Takte Vorspiel' in Act I, and in Act III a note '31 Takte Vorspiel, Lento' and a 3-bar lead-in revealing the use of the original prelude occur.

A letter dated 21 April 1904 to FD from Otto Mertens of the Stadttheater, Elberfeld, refers to this score, which Goldberg had had specially bound and interleaved.

(*f*). Vocal score by Eric Fenby, Boosey & Hawkes archives, pp. 188. Eng. words only; originally the words in Fenby's hand, but in some places altered in another hand. (The published words agree usually, but not always, with these alterations). This score is the basis of the published edition, v. inf., and all the music is in Fenby's autograph. *Note:* this vocal score by Eric Fenby has a different piano arrangement from that by Florent Schmitt.

(*g*). An autograph sheet of sketches, DT 39 f. 53 (RL 140), for parts of Act II; part reproduced in facsimile in DLP 33.

Libretti: Delius originally wrote the *music and the words at the same time*, according to his letter to Mrs. Jutta Bell of 25 February 1896. Some months later, he told her the text had been rewritten by C. F. Keary:

[Dec 1896] *I think that I told you that C. F. Keary wrote the libretto—We worked together & the result is all that I could wish.*

(α). Original version by C. F. Keary, Eng. only, Act II only, published in the programme of the Delius Orchestral Concert, 30 May 1899, pp. 25–34. MS of one leaf of Keary's original draft of a fragment from Act II, DT 39 f. 52 (RL 140), illustrated in DLP 33.

(β). Second version, Ger. only, as performed in Elberfeld, 30 March 1904, translated by Jelka Delius; 493 copies produced by Born-Verlag, Elberfeld, 1904. (I have been unable to see a copy of this publication: Mr. Fenby recalls it appeared to be a 'duplicated' production). Unsold copies 'held at the Composer's disposal' by Otto Mertens, see his letter 21 April 1904 to FD; subsequently untraced.

(γ). Typescript, Eng. only, basically of (α) but with gaps left where alterations were made for the 1904 performance. Into these gaps, a rough translation from (β) of the corresponding passages has been inserted in longhand (?by Jelka Delius) in Eng. This script is also in the Boosey & Hawkes archives, headed in longhand 'Words by C. F. Keary, Scenario and Music by Frederick Delius'. pp. 12, 7, 7.

(δ). Third version, Eng. only. 'Complete libretto. Text by C. F. Keary. Revised by Sir Thomas Beecham, Bart. and Edward Agate', Winthrop Rogers Edition, Boosey & Hawkes, pp. 23, n.d. [1935]. Typescript of this version, Boosey & Hawkes archives.

(ε). Fourth version, Eng. only. 'Revised libretto by Douglas Craig and Andrew Page', separately published only with EMI recording SLS 974, pp. 6–9, 1974, with introductory note, ibid. p. 5.

Publication: 1935, Winthrop Rogers Edition, Boosey & Hawkes 14331. Vocal score by Eric Fenby, Eng. only, pp. 157. Chorus parts 14332/3/4/5. (The music in this edition agrees with MS (*f*) above; the words with libretto (δ)).

1973, Vocal score reissued by Boosey & Hawkes in a limited (proof) edition only, including new libretto (ε) above and incorporating some corrections in the musical text.

1974, Vocal score, new edition, Boosey & Hawkes 20240, pp. [169]. Including the revised libretto by Douglas Craig and Andrew Page and incorporating some further corrections. In addition, this edition contains a 'Preface to the revised libretto of Koanga', pp. iii–viii, Publishers' note, p. ix, Appendix (i) 'Aria composed for the 1904 Elberfeld performance/ Reproduced in facsimile from Delius's MS', pp. 159–166, and Appendix (ii) 'Original prelude to Act III. Reproduced in facsimile/from the original vocal score by Florent Schmitt', pp. [167–169].

The engraving of the full score for publication is (1976) in hand with Boosey & Hawkes to plate no. 20349.

Performance: 30 May 1899, London, St. James's Hall, Delius Orchestral Concert, cond. Alfred Hertz. (Excerpts only: Prelude to Act III; Quintet and Finale of Act I; Act II [complete]).
Andrew Black (Koanga); Ella Russell (Palmyra).

30 March 1904 (and 2 subsequent performances), Elberfeld, Stadttheater, director Hans Gregor. Clarence Whitehill (Koanga), Rose Kaiser

(Palmyra), Georg Förster (Perez), Max Birkholz (Don José).
Cond: Fritz Cassirer; producer: Jacques Goldberg.

23 September 1935, London, Royal Opera House, Covent Garden.
John Brownlee (Koanga), Oda Slobodskaya (Palmyra), Frank Sale
(Perez), Leyland White (Don José).
London Philharmonic Orchestra, cond. Sir Thomas Beecham, Bart.

Story: From 'The Grandissimes: A Story of Creole Life', by George
Washington Cable, Scribners, New York, 1880. The episode in question,
concerning one 'Bras-Coupé', is to be found in Chaps. 28–29.

Arrangements: *Selection from the opera*, arranged by Eric Fenby for reduced
orchestra (2 (incl. Picc) 2. 2. BsCl. 2—4. 2. 3. 0—Timp. Tambno—Harp,
Banjos—Strings), MS, n.d. Boosey & Hawkes, pp. 40, unpubl. A note
pencilled on the score reads: 'The kernel of this work is contained in
"La Calinda" now published separately and much improved in
orchestration. E.F.' This selection is re-composed on material from the
following pages of the vocal score: 2; 15–18; 9 (last 2 lines) (all
transposed); the 'Calinda' (pp. 88–92 bar 7; 93 bar 11–95 last bar; 98);
127–8 (transposed); 151–154 (bar 4); 155 (last line)—end of opera.

La Calinda, dance from the opera, arranged by Eric Fenby. (Picc. 1. 2. 2.
2—4. 2. 3. 1 (ad lib)—Timp. Cym. Trgl. Tambno—Harp, Banjos (ad
lib)—Strings).
1938, Boosey & Hawkes 8061, full score, and later (1946) included in
HPS 86, 9065, miniature score, pp. 22.
(MS Boosey & Hawkes archives; also a different MS of the
corresponding movement extracted from the *Florida* Suite, q.v.). This is a
purely orchestral recomposition (for reduced orchestra) of the relevant
section from Act II, omitting 21 bars at cue no. 14 and ending with the
andante bars which close *Florida*, part 1.

1947, Boosey & Hawkes 15777, arranged for 2 pianos by Joan Trimble,
pp. 12.

1949, Boosey & Hawkes 16582, piano reduction by Harold Perry, pp. 7.

1976, arranged by Eric Fenby, for flute and piano or flute and string
orchestra, for James Galway.

Note: none of these versions of 'La Calinda' includes the delightful
contrapuntal effect of the combination of the negro chorus with the
Calinda theme on its last occurrence in the opera. By a happy chance,
the earliest sketch of these very bars survives in DT 39 f 53 b (RL 140)
see DLP 33.

Intermezzo from Koanga, arranged by Stanford Robinson for reduced
orchestra (3. 2. CA. 2. BsCl. 3—4. 2. 3. 1—Timp. Perc.—Harp—Strings),
MS BBC unpubl. This excerpt commences with the last 9 bars of p. 1 of
the vocal score, and is then based on the transformation music from the
Prologue (cue 2 until 2 bars after cue 4) and end of Act III (bar 6 of p. 150
to the pause on p. 154).

Beecham used to perform the *Closing Scene from Koanga* in concert
form, consisting of the transformation music at the end of Act III,
commencing just after cue 40 on p. 151, and proceeding to the end of
the opera. A cut of 29 bars after the pause (pp. 154–5) was made.

31

Notes: TB 81–3, 85, 93–4, 99–100, 124–5, 130; EF 95–6, 112; CD 145–7; RL 141. Chop 19 lists the work as item 5. See also William Randel, '*Koanga* and its libretto', *Music and Letters*, Vol. 52 no. 2 (April 1971), pp. 141–156; Robert Threlfall, 'The Early History of *Koanga*', *Tempo* 110 (September 1974), pp. 8–11.

An earlier version of the music of *La Calinda* occurs in the first movement of the orchestral *Florida Suite*, q.v. The prelude to Act III, as published, was transferred unaltered from the opera *The Magic Fountain*, where the same passage had served as prelude to Act II.
Sir Thomas Beecham, in his 1935 performances, used the orchestral *Irmelin Prelude* (q.v.) as an orchestral interlude in Act III, at cue no. 20.
The old (copyist's) MS orchestral material, in the Boosey Opera Library, includes the original parts used for the extracts given at the 1899 London concert—in the hand of the 'Paris copyist'. These reveal that, even as early as that occasion, the 'Prelude to Act III' was in fact the transplanted *Magic Fountain* excerpt.

I/5 FOLKERAADET
Incidental music to Gunnar Heiberg's satiric Drama

(Zwischenacts Musik zu G.H.'s satirischem Drama Folkeraadet)—[MS score]
Suite for Orchestra [MS—Norwegian Suite]
'(Composed for the satiric drama "The Council of the People", by Gunnar Heiberg)' [1899 programme]
There are four principal movements, viz:

    I. 'Vorspiel 1ste Akt'. Bewegt (C major) pp. 17
    II. Lustig bewegt   (G major) pp. 28
  No. 3 Allegro energico   (C major) pp. 30
    IV. Marcia, lento solenne   (C min.–maj.) pp. 27

There are also two short passages of incidental music, one for Act 2 and one for Act 5.

Date: 1897. Signature on MS (*Frederick D.*) evidently added later.

Orchestra: 2. 2. 2. 2—4. 2. 3 (Tenors). 1—Timp. BD. Cym. Tambour (Kleine Trommel)—Strings.

> Pencilled into the MS of the last two movements is an enhanced orchestration; probably dating from the 1899 concert performance, when these extra instruments were available anyway (and the programme note confirms the woodwind accordingly as 3. 3. 3. 4). At the end of the third movement also, a part for a third trumpet is introduced.

MS: (*a*) Autograph full score, DT 13 ff 1–56 (RL 60–65), dated, and signed (see above).

> (*b*). Short score sketches, DT 39 ff 61–2 (RL 142); f 61a is for the separate passage for Act 2, f 62b for that for Act 5 and a fragment used in No. 3. ff 61b–62a show contrapuntal developments of cognate, but not identical, material.

> (*c*). Copyist's full score, ?Beecham Library.

Publication: none. Facsimile of p. 1 of autograph full score, RL 60 (plate 17).

Performance: 18 October 1897 et seq., Christiania (Oslo), Christiania Theatre, cond. Per Winge (and not Delius, as has been stated more than once).
30 May 1899, London, St. James's Hall, Alfred Hertz, movements 3–4 only.
12 January 1974, London, BBC Concert Orchestra cond. Ashley Lawrence, complete (for broadcast on 29 January 1974).

Notes: PW 37–9 (53–4); TB 97–8.
Chop 19 lists the work as item 4.
RL (loc. cit. and Appendix 5) gives further detail of the circumstances surrounding the first performance.
Play:
Gunnar Heiberg (1857–1929): *Folkeraadet*, Komedie i fem Akter (1897)

I/6 A VILLAGE ROMEO AND JULIET
Romeo und Julia auf dem Dorfe
Lyrisches Drama in 6 Bildern nach Gottfried Keller.

Date: 1900–01 (according to third [UE] edition of the vocal score); as early as 28 January 1898, however, FD writing to Jelka Rosen sends the libretto for her to read and give her opinion. Runciman, op. cit., says 'finished in 1900', and gives title as 'The Garden of Paradise'. CD 200: 'When I was staying with him in Elberfeld in 1905 [sic: ?1904] he was still working on the score, polishing and making alterations'.

Characters: Manz ⎫
                Marti ⎬ rich farmers
Sali, son of Manz
Vrenchen, daughter of Marti
The Dark [Black (1st edition)] Fiddler, Right Heir to the Wildland
1, 2 Peasants
1, 2, 3 [Peasant] Women
Gingerbread Woman
Wheel-of-Fortune Woman
Cheap Jewellery Woman
Showman
Merry-go-round Man
Shooting-gallery Man
Vagabonds:
    The Slim Girl; the Wild Girl;
    The Poor Horn-Player;
    The Hunchbacked Bass-Fiddler
1, 2, 3 Bargees
Vagabonds, Peasants and Bargees.

Scenes: 1 (orig. The Prologue, scenes 1–3). September. A piece [strip] of land . . . on a hill.
    2 (orig. Act I scene 1). Six years later. Outside Marti's house.
    3 (orig. Act I scenes 2–4). The Wildland.
    4 (orig. Act II). Interior of Marti's house.
    The dream of Sali and Vrenchen.
    5 (orig. Act III scenes 1–3). The Fair.
    ('Szenenwechsel'). The Walk to the Paradise Garden.
    6 (orig. Act III scenes 4–5). The Paradise Garden.

Place of action: Seldwyla, Switzerland.
Time: Middle of the nineteenth century. Six [orig. eight] years elapse between the First and Second Scenes.

Orchestra: 3 (incl. Picc). 3. CA. 3. BsCl. 3. Contra—6. 3. 3 (Tenors). 1 —Timp. Xyl. Tamt. Cym. 3 Bells. Glockenspiel—2 Harps—Strings.

On the stage: Soloviolin ⎫ ad lib. ⎰ (scenes 1, 3 & 6)
             6 Horns   ⎭ in Orch. ⎱ (scenes 3 & 6)
            'Stahlplatten', 2 Church Bells, Organ (scene 4)
            2 Cornets, 2 Alto Trb., Tenor Drum (scene 5)

MS: (*a*). Autograph full score, ? originally Harmonie-Verlag according to the terms of the contract, present whereabouts untraced.

(*b*). Vocal score by Florent Schmitt, DT 19 ff 1–103 (RL 76–78), entitled *Le Jardin du Paradis*. The piano part, in mauve ink, is in Schmitt's hand, the voice parts being in Delius's hand. Eng. words and stage directions principally in FD's hand; French translation in red ink below, and Ger. trans. of words drafted above in pencil, the latter in Jelka Delius's hand. [The Fr. trans. is known to be by Robert d'Humières, v. LKC 75]. There are considerable overworkings to the voice part and words.

Undated, this score appears to be the earliest surviving version of the work, and is divided into a Prologue and 3 Acts. A number of passages were subsequently altered, v. inf., and the interlude 'The Walk to the Paradise Garden' added in place of a shorter entr'acte, *see Plates 4–5*. The Eng. words (and most of the stage directions) in this copy agree on the whole with those later published in the Harmonie full score, cf. inf., with the notable exception of the stage directions for the opening of the last scene. (These agree with the earliest, separately published, Eng. libretto (β) inf., but go on to say: 'they all have the air of awaiting with interest something the fiddler is about to tell them'). Facsimile of p. 70 from Act II of this MS, DLP 46.

Libretti: FD sent a libretto of the work ('Romeo & Julie') from Paris to Jelka Rosen, then in Grez, in 1898 (v. letter 28 January 1898, original in Grainger Museum). An undated letter from C. F. Keary shows that he also was at one time working on a libretto for this work. Writing to Ernest Newman on 19 August 1929, however, Delius wrote, in reference to this opera . . . *the words for which I made myself and in* English, *of course. This work also was first performed and published* [sic] *in Berlin, and my wife then translated it into German to the music.* See also Chop, 18, 'Bearbeitung des Librettos vom Komponisten'. No edition of the text or music specifically states who was the author of the English libretto.

(α[1]). The first published version of the libretto is the German text included in the first edition of the lithographed vocal score, ca. 1906, v. inf. Not only differing from the separately-issued libretti listed below, this is also often very incomplete as regards stage directions.

(α[2]). Romeo und Julia auf dem Dorfe (Frei nach Gottfried Keller's gleichnamiger Erzählung). (Aus dem Englischen übersetzt von Jelka-Rosen). Musikdrama in einem Vorspiel und drei Aufzügen von FD, ptd. Albert Beyer, Berlin II, Usedomstr. 17, pp. 43 [?1907], Ger. only. This text differs in a number of places from α[1], but agrees on the whole with that published in the Harmonie scores of 1910 (which omit a few lines from 'Act II', however); but the stage directions are still often in an earlier form, though amplified from those in α[1]. The directions at the opening of the last scene agree with those in the MS vocal score (b) above, but omit the last few clauses thereof; between scenes 3 and 4 of Act III appears the single word 'Szenenwechsel'.

FD's letter of 26 December 1908 to Harmonie, speaking of the preparation of the printed vocal score by that company, refers to *Rumpel's text . . . which does not agree with the libretto at all* (cf. RL 77). Further information on this does not appear to be forthcoming.

(β). A Village Romeo and Juliet. A Music Drama in Six Scenes by Frederick Delius. The Text founded on the Novel of Gottfried Keller. [London]. pp. 27, [1910]—n.d. but BL Cat. thus—Eng. only; no

Plates 4–5: Le Jardin du Paradis [A Village Romeo and Juliet].
Vocal score by Florent Schmitt.
The original version of the interlude between the last two scenes.

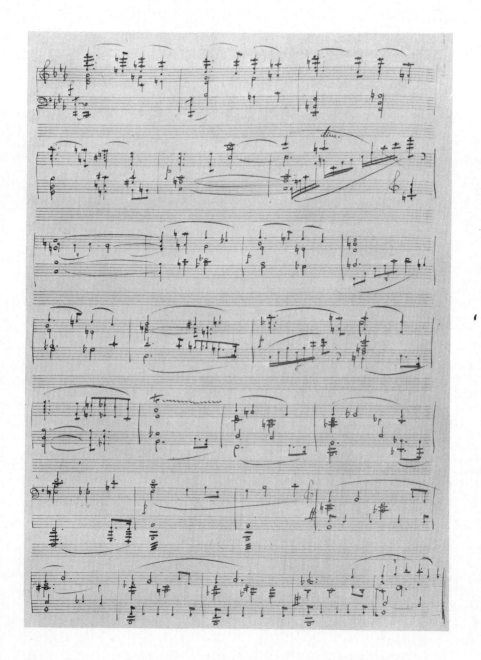

Plate 5

publisher's name. This libretto agrees (with minimal differences) with the English text appearing in the Harmonie scores.

(γ). Romeo und Julia auf dem Dorfe . . . Lyrisches Drama in sechs Bildern. Copyright 1910 by „Harmonie" Berlin, Universal Edition 6929, pp. 31 [?1921]. Ger. only. This text agrees basically with that of α² above, less some cuts, but the stage directions are now further extended and altered, agreeing with those found in the later editions of the vocal score as issued by UE in 1921 and after; in particular with reference to the opening of the last scene and the interlude preceding same.

(δ). FD. A Village Romeo and Juliet, Lyrical Music Drama in 6 scenes from the novel by Gottfried Keller. Copyright 1910 by Harmonie Berlin W, Universal Edition no. 6929a, pp. 31 [?193..], Eng. only. Printed in Great Britain by Knight & Sons, Woking. Publishers: Universal Edition, Vienna; London Agents: Cranz & Co. Ltd., 40 Langham St. W.1. [Cranz and Co. were London agents for UE from 1 September 1931; the previous agents—from 1922—were Curwen & Sons]. This libretto agrees with the English words and stage directions found in the UE vocal score of 1921.

(ε). New English version by Tom Hammond. (This version was used for the 1962 revival). Issued 'for distribution only with Long Play Records nos. SAN 316–318 (SLS 966)', pp. 5–6, 8–10, 1973.

Publication: [ca. 1906] 'Romeo und Julie auf dem Dorfe (nach Gottfried Keller's gleichnamiger Erzählung). Musikdrama in Einem Prolog und drei Akten'. Propriété de l'Auteur, Paris. Lévy-Lulx, autographiste; 6 Impasse Marie-Blanche, Paris (18ᵉ). *Vocal score* with Ger. words only, pp. 109. The piano part agrees with that in the MS vocal score arrangement by Florent Schmitt; the score as a whole follows that same MS (b) fairly closely, the sense of the stage directions, though largely incomplete, agreeing therewith.

A copy in BL, K.5. d. 1, marked 'Partie: der Schwarze Geiger' and 'Eingerichtet' was that used by the performer of the Dark Fiddler's part at the première in Berlin in 1907.

Another copy, now in the archive of the DT, was that used by Ruth Vincent, performer of the part of Vrenchen at the London première in 1910; it bears her performing marks, and an Eng. translation of her part is added in red ink, largely in the hand of Sir Thomas Beecham (Note: this latter translation differs from all the published Eng. libretti).

Another copy was sent to the Mondelli Theatre, Florence, with a covering letter dated 10 June 1907 from FD (RL 78).

A further copy, uninscribed, is in the Bodleian Library, Oxford, Mus. 22c. 793.

The first three of these copies are all marked with minor cuts and alterations; but only the Mondelli copy also has a MS insertion of the extended version of the interlude between the present scenes 5 and 6 now known as *The Walk to the Paradise Garden*, which is thus seen to date from 1907 at the latest. Whether it was written before the first performance that year, or subsequently when staging may have revealed the need for such an extension, is not certain; but the former seems more probable. (v. inf. for further details relating).

Note: FD to Bantock, 26 October 1910, says . . . *performance of the Village Romeo & Juliet which Beecham is going to give again. As the last performance was given under such bad auspices. No piano scores—no text books etc.* (This explains why Ruth Vincent, and presumably her colleagues too, worked from copies of this 'Paris version').

1910, 'Romeo und Julia auf dem Dorfe. Lyrisches Drama in sechs Bildern nach Gottfried Keller'. *Full score*, Verlag Harmonie 449, Ger. and Eng. words, lithographed, pp. 179. 'Autographie und Druck von C. G. Röder, GmbH, Leipzig'. *Vocal score*, ditto, 'Musikalisch lyrisches Drama . . . Klavierauszug von Otto Lindemann'. Verlag Harmonie 1010, Ger. and Eng. words, pp. 246, 'Stich u. Druck: Berliner Musikalien Druckerei'; cover lithoed by Röder, 'Titelzeichnung und Buchschmuck v. P. Telemann' (Facsimile in DLP 58). This piano arrangement differs completely from the above first edition of ca. 1906.

A number of musical changes were made in these definitive editions, of which the most important are as follows (ref. to this vocal score): minor alts. on pp. 7, 9, 13, 14, 22, 23, 24, 28;
p. 40: the last 6 bars replace 11 different bars, which originally finished the first scene in G flat major.
minor alts. on pp. 49, 82, 104;
p. 108: 25 bars deleted after bar 4.
minor alts. on pp. 133, 170;
p. 183, Cue 39 to foot of p. 189. Originally, in the MS vocal score (b) and the first printed vocal score of ca. 1906, a much shorter interlude, only 45 bars long and remaining in and around the key of E flat, occurred here (*see plates 4–5*).

It is often stated (not, however, by Beecham) that a suggestion from Beecham to Delius initiated the composition of the beautiful extended interlude, now so justly famous as 'The Walk to the Paradise Garden'. The evidence given in RL 78, and summarized above, concerning the Mondelli copy of the first edition and its dated covering letter, proves that this music existed before Beecham and FD first met (which was after Cassirer's performance of *Appalachia* in London in November 1907, MC 63), indeed before Beecham ever heard the opera at all. (The list of biographical details in the programme of the 3rd concert of the 1929 Delius Festival states that the interlude in question was composed in 1906). In MC 88–9 however Beecham did specifically refer to introducing 'a new stage picture' [to stop the audience talking!] during the performance of this lengthy entr'acte 'when I revived the work some years later' (i.e. in 1920). Delius's own copy of the full score, now in the DT archive, has some extra stage directions in his own hand, pencilled in during rehearsal at this point on p. 135.

1921, Transferred to Universal Edition, Vienna. *Vocal score* by Otto Lindemann, subsequently reissued as UE 3912. (There are a very few further alterations to the music in this edition, e.g. p. 82: 5 bars deleted after bar 9; p. 108: bars 5–7 inserted). The piano part is otherwise the same as in the Harmonie vocal score of 1910, but the Eng. words differ somewhat. Also, a number of stage directions are added (e.g. those during the interlude between the last 2 scenes) or amplified (e.g. the different grouping and the Dark Fiddler's stance at the beginning of the last scene). It appears from a letter from Philip Heseltine to Cecil Gray

on 19 November 1921 (Gray 243) that Heseltine was (at least in part)
responsible for these changes ('I have also re-translated the *Village
Romeo* for a new edition').
Note: the words 'Der Gang nach dem Paradiesgarten' now for the first
time appear, on p. 183.

1952, Transferred to Boosey & Hawkes Limited, London. *Vocal score*
(as UE 3912) reprinted and first issued as B & H 19032 in 1964.

1973, *Study score*, B & H 20136 (HPS 885) issued. 'This edition is a
reprint in reduced format of the full score originally published by
Harmonie Verlag, Berlin, in 1910 (No. 449)'.

Performance: 21 February 1907 (and two other performances), Berlin,
Komisches Oper; dir. Hans Gregor.
Willi Merkel (Sali), Lola Artôt de Padilla (Vrenchen).
Desider Zador (The Dark Fiddler).
Cond: Fritz Cassirer.

22 February 1910, London, Royal Opera House, Covent Garden ('The
Village Romeo and Juliet').
Walter Hyde (Sali), Ruth Vincent (Vrenchen), Robert Maitland (The
Dark Fiddler).
Cond. Thomas Beecham.

Story: Gottfried Keller (1819–1890), Romeo und Julia auf dem Dorfe, from
Die Leute von Seldwyla (first series, 1856).

Arrangements: [?1913] *The Walk to the Paradise Garden* from the music
drama . . . Der Gang nach dem Paradiesgarten aus dem lyrischen Drama
. . . [piano solo, extract from Otto Lindemann's vocal score, i.e. p. 183
cue 39 to foot of p. 189 with minor alterations, viz: no cue numbers or
stage directions; modified at cues 49–50, 5 bars at 51, and from 52 to 4
bars after 53]. UE 3555, pp. 7. FD to Jelka Delius, Oct. 1913 . . . *he*
[Hertzka] *edits separately the V.R. & J. entr'acte.*

1934, Intermezzo. The Walk . . . Entr'acte from . . . Der Gang . . .
Zwischenaktsmusik aus . . ., 'slightly rearranged for performance by
concert orchestra' by Keith Douglas (2. 2 (CA). 2. 2—4. 2. 3 (2 Ten. 1
Bass). 0—Timp.—Harp (PF)—Strings), full score, UE 10579, pp. 20.
(This version begins at full score cue 38 of the opera).

1940, Ditto. Intermezzo from . . . arranged by Sir Thomas Beecham.
'This arrangement has been made in order to bring the work within the
scope of smaller orchestras'. (2. 1. CA. 2. 2—4. 2. 3 (2 Ten. 1 Bass). 0
—Timp.—Harp—Strings), full score, B & H 8375, pp. 17; later
(1941–2) miniature score B & H 8658, included in HPS 23 (Three
orchestral pieces). (This version begins at full score cue 39 of the opera).

1950, Ditto. Arranged by Harold Perry for piano solo, B & H 16952,
pp. 7.

For use of this work in ballet, see below.

1939, *Waltz* 'slightly rearranged for performance by concert orchestra' by
Keith Douglas (2 (Picc). 2 (CA). 2. 2—4. 2. 3 (2 Ten. 1 Bass). 0—Timp.
Bells, Glockenspiel. Trgl. T. Mil. Cym—Harp (PF) ad lib.—Strings), full
score UE 11106, pp. 49. This is a condensed orchestral version of the
fairground music from scene 5, with an optional link whereby the Waltz

may be followed, as in the opera, by the 'Walk to the Paradise Garden'. The following bars of the score of scene 5 are here omitted: from 4 bars after cue 13 to cue 16; from cues 17 to 18; from 7 bars after cue 31 to cue 33.

Note following performances of excerpts:
14 February 1912 'Entr'acte from V.R. & J', Birmingham Philharmonic Society, Beecham.
24 November 1914 'Walk to the Paradise Garden' [so titled], preceded by 'Dance at the Fair', London, Queen's Hall, Philharmonic Society, Beecham.
The excerpts given at the opening concert of the 1929 Delius Festival consisted of (a) The Fair; (b) Walk to the Paradise Garden; (c) Closing Scene.

1933, *Wedding Music*/Hochzeitsmusik from the opera . . . Arranged by Eric Fenby for chorus (S.A.T.B.B.) and organ, UE 10458, pp. 4.

[1948]. *Suite* from . . . arranged by Eric Fenby. (2 (incl. Picc). 2 (incl. CA). 2. BsCl (opt.). 2—4. 2. 3. 1—Timp. Xyl. Bells. Cym. Tamt. T. Mil. —Harp—Strings). MS, Boosey & Hawkes, pp. 34, unpubl.
  (i) The Dark Fiddler (part transposed, recomposed and condensed from Scene 1, cues 17 to 26).
  (ii) The Dream of Sali and Vrenchen (recomposed and condensed from Scene 4, cues 31–38, 42).
  (iii) The Fair (recomposed, part transposed and condensed from Scene 5, beginning to cue 13 and cues 35–6 with free conclusion).

Arrangements for ballet use:
Romeo and Juliet, a ballet by Antony Tudor, Ballet Theatre, Metropolitan Opera House, New York, 6 April 1943. The music consists of the following works: *Over the hills and far away, The Walk to the Paradise Garden, Eventyr, Irmelin Prelude* and *Brigg Fair*. They are played complete except for small cuts in Eventyr and Brigg Fair. 'The music . . . was arranged [for pit orchestra] by the conductor of the company Antal Dorati. Some of the New York performances were directed by Sir Thomas Beecham'. (v. *Tempo* 7, London, June 1944, p. 19). Perf. London, 1946, New York Ballet Theatre, Covent Garden (Antony Tudor, Nora Kaye, Hugh Laing).
The Walk to the Paradise Garden was used (complete) for a ballet of the same title by Sir Frederick Ashton, Royal Ballet, Covent Garden, 15 November 1972 (Merle Park, David Wall, Derek Rencher).

Notes: PW 80–90 (83–90); CD 183–186; MC 88, 178–9; TB 139–142, 156–8, 188; RL 76–78, 142–3. Chop 19 lists the work as item 8.

A copy of the printed full score bearing Sir Thomas Beecham's markings is now in the DT Archive.

New performing material on transparent masters was produced by Boosey & Hawkes (no. 20136) in 1973 for their Opera Library, to replace the sole original MS set.

A reduced orchestration (3 (Picc). 2 (CA). 2 (Bass). 2 (Contra)—4. 2. 3. 1—Timp.—Perc.—Harp—Strings) was prepared in 1973 by Igor Buketoff for St. Paul Opera; this version was also used by the Washington Opera Company for their performances.

I/7 MARGOT LA ROUGE
Drame lyrique en 1 Acte
Paroles de Rosenval

Date: 1901–2. The *Idyll* (q.v.), using material from *Margot*, is dated 1901;
a copy of the printed score of *Margot* bears the note in Delius's hand:
finished April 1902, v. inf.

Personnages: Le Sergent Thibault
  L'Artiste
  Lapoigne
  Totor
  1er 2e Soldats
  1er 2e 3e Buveurs
  un Garçon (limonadier)
  Le Brigadier de Police
  Margot
  Lili Béguin
  Nini
  La Patronne
  1e 2e Femmes
  Filles, Consommateurs, Agents de Police.

Scène: Un cabaret des boulevards. Il est huit heures du soir. C'est la fin du
  printemps.

Orchestra: presumed to be the same as used for the *Idyll* (q.v.), viz: 2. 2.
  CA. 2. 2—4. 2. 3. 1—Timp.—Harp—Strings. (This assumption is
  confirmed by Eric Fenby's recollection).

MS: (*a*) One page (the last, paginated 73) of a pencil draft vocal score in
  Delius's own hand, DT 39 f 66 (RL 143), differing in both words and
  music from the definitive version, *see plates 6 and 7*.

  (*b*). Autograph full score untraced at present, but used by Eric Fenby
  when working on the *Idyll* in 1932, and shown by him on 1935/1 list as
  'Margot la Rouge—Drame lyric—1902'.

  (*c*). Vocal score by Maurice Ravel, DT 20 (RL 79–81), pp. 48. The music
  is almost entirely in Ravel's hand (except for a few bars which, as they
  were not clear to him, he left blank, illus. in DLP 48, for Delius to fill in).
  French words and stage directions also in Ravel's hand; Italian ditto, in
  red ink, added beneath in a hand still unidentified.

Publication: ca. 1905, Propriété des Auteurs, Paris. Autogr: Lévy-Lulx,
  Paris (18e) 6 Impasse Marie-Blanche. Imp: Crevel F^{res}, F^g St Denis, 18,
  Paris. Partition Piano et Chant; French words only, pp. 69. The piano
  part agrees with the MS arrangement by Maurice Ravel, though there are
  some minor engraver's errors. (See below for some details of MS
  corrections and alterations in this vocal score). Facsimile of p. 1 of
  Ravel's autograph, RL 80 (plate 21); of pp. 3–4, LKC 57–8; of p. 29,
  DLP 48; (FD has completed some bars left blank by Ravel).

Performance: none. The work was composed for and entered in the
  Concorso Melodrammatico Internationale of 1904, sponsored by the
  publisher Sonzogno of Milan (not by Ricordi, as sometimes stated).

Notes: PW 101–2 (97–8); TB 121–2; EF 118–9; RL 79–82. Chop 20 lists the work as item 9, 'Eine Nacht in Paris: Musiktragödie in einen Aufzuge'.

Several copies of the published vocal score have been examined and compared: in many of them a number of alterations and additions have been made in ink, probably in FD's hand.

(i) DT 21 (RL 82). Inscribed with his name and date (1932) by Eric Fenby. No alterations to the text.

(ii) BL K.7.g. 16. *To my friend Philip Heseltine . . . 28/3/1913*. Heseltine has noted on the first page of the music 'piano score transcribed by Maurice Ravel'. There are a number of corrections (to agree with Ravel's MS), also alterations and additions, especially on pp. 32–4, 40 and 51 (cf. RL 166).

(iii) Coll: Albi Rosenthal. Inscribed: *To John Coates with kindest greetings from Frederick Delius . . . 15th Dec 1907*, and *finished April 1902*. Various corrections and alterations, but not the major ones as on pp. 32–3 of (ii). Facsimile of titlepage, DLP 59.

(iv) Birmingham University, Department of Music, M 1503.D. *To my friend Granville Bantock . . . 1908*. This has most of the above-noted alterations, including those on pp. 32–3.

(v) Oxford, Bodleian Library, Mus. 22d. 1066. No inscription. Most of the above alterations, but not those on pp. 32–3.

(vi) York University, Music Library; unmarked.

The identification of the librettist, 'Rosenval', as Berthe Gaston-Danville was established by LKC 59.

See entry under *Idyll* for Soprano, baritone and orchestra (II/10, p. 72) for later use of the same music.

FD's interest in writing a dramatic one-act opera did not cease with the completion of *Margot*: he next (1902–3) very seriously considered basing such a work on *Salomé*, Oscar Wilde's original one-act French drama of 1893; for permission to use which he commenced negotiation, before sole operatic rights in this project were gained by Richard Strauss for his world-famous score of 1904–5. (see TB 122).

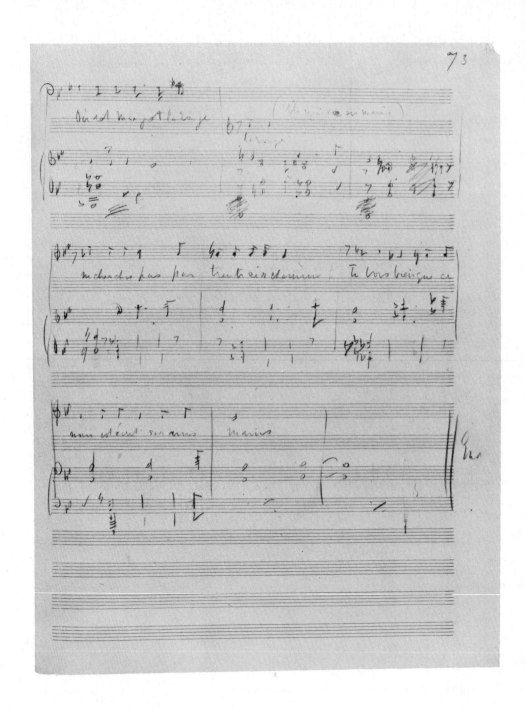

Plate 6: Margot la Rouge. Last page of early draft vocal score

Plate 7: Margot la Rouge. Last page of printed vocal score

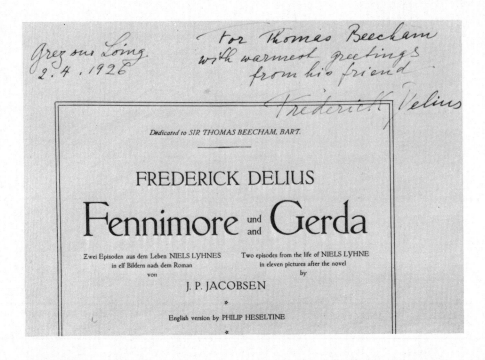

Plate 8: Fennimore and Gerda
(a) dedicatory inscription on titlepage of published full score, in Jelka Delius's hand.

(b) page of music added at commencement

I/8 FENNIMORE AND GERDA

Two episodes from the life of Niels Lyhne in eleven pictures after the novel by J. P. Jacobsen set to music by FD. (Zwei Episoden aus dem Leben Niels Lyhnes in elf Bildern nach dem Roman von J. P. J. Musik-Bühnenspiel von FD).

Date: 1909–10, according to the MS full score. Most authorities give 1908–10. FD to Bantock, 11 April 1911: *I am putting finishing touches to Niels Lyhne.*

Dedication: 'Dedicated to Sir Thomas Beecham, Bart.' (on printed full score only; titlepage of MS lost).

Characters: Consul Claudi
  His wife
  Fennimore, their daughter
  Niels Lyhne ⎫ cousins; Claudi's nephews
  Erik Refstrup ⎭
  Five boon companions (A Sportsman; a Town Councillor; a Tutor; a Distiller; a Doctor [dumb role])
  Councillor Skinnerup
  Gerda ⎫ his daughters
  Ingrid, Lila, Marit ⎭
  Maidservant, Girls and Farmhands
  Tenor voice (on the water)

Scenes: 1–2 pictures, at Consul Claudi's house at Fjordby
  3–9 pictures, at Mariagerfjord where Erik and Fennimore live after their wedding.
  10 picture, at Niels Lyhne's estate at Lönborggaard.
  11 picture, in Councillor Skinnerup's garden, almost a year later.

Three years elapse between 2 & 3 and 9 & 10.

At the end of 2 in full score and MS vocal score: 'End of the first Act'.

Orchestra: 3 (incl. Picc). 2. CA. BsOb [tacet in 10–11]. 3. BsCl. 3. Sarrusophone (Contra)—4. 3. 3. 1—Timp. Trgl. Cym. Glockenspiel—2 Harps—Strings.
  4 Horns 'on the stage' in scene 6.

MS: (*a*) Autograph full score, Universal Edition Archiv, now BL Loan 54/2, 1909–10, lacking titlepage, pp. [217]; Ger. text only, but a few pencillings indicate points for the proposed Eng. translation. There are some violet ink minor alterations and corrections (?by the publisher's reader) and some red crayon changes to dynamics. The remarks at the ends of the scenes, specifying the length of the pauses to be observed, are also in red crayon. In part, the score is ink over pencil. Towards the very end, some of the tempi are indicated in Eng. and Ger.
This MS full score lacks bars 1–3 of the printed editions (which are to be found, in a copyist's hand, separately in DT 39 f 110 (RL 149) headed 'Anfang der Oper' *see plate 8*). Two bars between cues 32 and 33 are rewritten as three (now bars 4–6 after cue 32) on an inserted sheet; so are the last 7 attacca bars at the end of the 8th picture (which originally finished on the A minor chord). The heading 'Bild VIII' originally stood

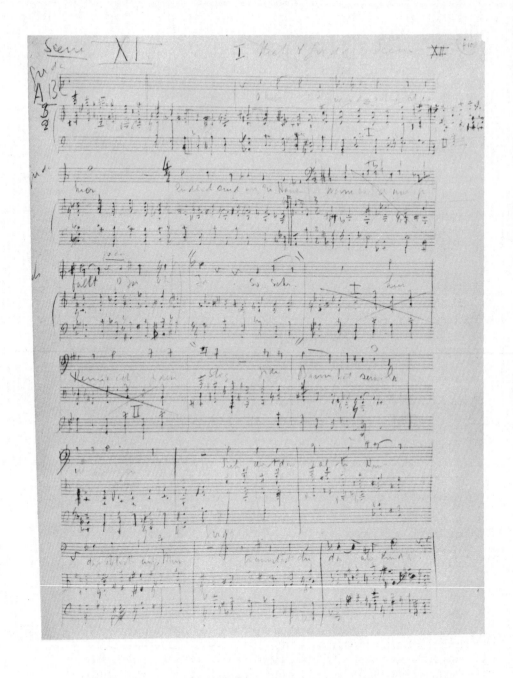

Plate 9: Fennimore and Gerda. A page for a rejected 'Scene XII'

5 bars after cue 83 and was marked back with arrows to 2 bars before cue 82.

(*b*). Vocal score in the bold hand of an unidentified professional copyist, with a few pencilled corrections, ('Klavierauszug von Otto Lindemann'), coll: R. Threlfall, pp. 170, Ger. words only. This score has all the cue numbers, but lacks the first 3 bars, also the link between 8–9 pictures and the alterations between cues 32 and 33. It also lacks the details of instrumentation (meticulously entered in the published vocal score) and the timings of the pauses between the scenes; and indicates the start of scene 8 16 bars later than in the printed vocal scores, v. supra.
It appears that this MS was made before actual performance showed the practical necessity of the opening bars (to get the curtain up) and the desirability of linking scenes 8–9. It may have been intended as the original *Stichvorlage* for the vocal score, though it lacks engraver's marks, etc.

(*c*). Extensive rough sketches for the opera, some referring to later scenes of the novel not in fact used in the finished work, are to be found in DT 39 ff 95–110 (RL 147–9). Facsimile of a passage from 'Gerda' in DLP 74. A rejected page for 'Scene XII', *see plate 9*.

Publication: 1919, Fennimore und Gerda. Oper in 11 Bildern.
Libretto, Ger. only, Universal Edition 6306, pp. [24].
Vocal score by Otto Lindemann; two separate editions, viz. Universal Edition 6305 (Ger. only) and 6308 (English version by Philip Heseltine), pp. 83. The front cover carries a Munch-like crayon drawing (unattributed— ?by Jelka Delius) depicting the scene at the end of the second picture, see DLP 74 and sleeve of record set SLS 991.
In 'patching' the Eng. directions and words over the Ger. originals for printing as 6308, the latter have not always been completely obscured. At the same time, some uncorrected errors and missed accidentals have crept into the voice parts while altering the declamation to suit the Eng. trans.

1926, *Full score*, Universal Edition 7925, Ger. and Eng. words, pp. 140. 'Dedicated to Sir Thomas Beecham Bart.' In this full score, the start of scene 7 is at cue 68+2 (instead of at cue 69+7, as in the vocal score). The orchestral material is marked to agree. (A copy now in the DT Archive bears an inscription from Composer to dedicatee, in Jelka Delius's hand, dated 2. 4. 1926 *see plate 8*. This copy also has Beecham's markings in scenes 10–11).

1952, Copyright assigned to Boosey & Hawkes Ltd.

1976, *Study score*, Boosey & Hawkes 20326 (HPS 896) issued. 'This edition is a reprint in reduced format of the full score originally published by Universal-Edition, Vienna, in 1926 (Universal-Edition Nr. 7925)'.

Performance: A performance in Cologne in 1914 was proposed but abandoned (see memo of conversation by G. Tischer dated 1 July 1913, filed with the contract; also FD to Bantock, 27 March 1914: *my new music Drama—Fennimore & Gerda will be given next October in Cologne*).

21 October 1919, Frankfurt am Main, Opernhaus;
Robert van Scheidt (Niels)
Emma Holt (Fennimore)

Erik Wirl (Erik)
Elisabeth Kandt (Gerda)
Cond: Gustav Brecher; scenery, Walter Brügmann.

24 October 1929, London, Queen's Hall, *Gerda* only; Royal
Philharmonic Orchestra, Pauline Maunder, John Goss; cond: Sir Thos.
Beecham.

27 March 1962, London, broadcast, BBC Third Programme. John
Cameron (Niels), Sybil Michelow (Fennimore), Max Worthley (Erik),
Jeanette Sinclair (Gerda). Cond: Stanford Robinson.

23–24 May 1968, Hammersmith Municipal Opera, Old Town Hall,
Fulham Broadway. Robert Bateman (Niels), Carolyn Maia (Fennimore),
Jack Irons (Erik), Audrey Attwood (Gerda). Cond: Joseph Vandernoot.
Prod: Basil Ashmore.

Story: Jens Peter Jacobsen (1847–1885): Niels Lyhne (1880). German
libretto by the composer, presumably based on the Ger. trans. of
Jacobsen's novel. FD to Ernest Newman, 19 August 1929: *You know how
difficult it is to translate to music. This is the reason why in composing
"Fennimore & Gerda" and the "Arabesk"—to avoid a language like
Danish, which has no public—I composed to german words.*

Arrangements: 1945 'Intermezzo' [arranged by Eric Fenby from the preludes
to scenes 10–11]. (2. 1. CA. 2. 2—2. 1. 0. 0—Strings). Boosey & Hawkes
9000 full score, and later (1946) included in HPS 86, 9065, miniature
score ('Three orchestral pieces') pp. 23–33. MS, in Eric Fenby's
autograph, Boosey archives, pp. 5.

Notes: PW 92–100 (91–7); CD 199–200; TB 163–5, 185–7.
The original (copyist's) MS orchestral material is in the Boosey Opera
Library. This exhibits the same alterations—the added 3 bars at the
opening; the rewriting between cues 32 & 33; the setting back of the
starts of scenes 7 and 8; and the link between scenes 8 and 9—as the
autograph full score. These changes, then, evidently date from the time of
the first performance in 1919. A cut from cue 105 − 1 to 106 + 4 was also
marked into this material at some time undetermined.

During the period of delay in staging the first performance due to the first
War, FD is authoritatively said to have been considering basing further
music dramas on 'Wuthering Heights' and 'Deirdre of the Sorrows'.
See PW 102 (98); CD 196–7.

I/9 HASSAN
Drama in 5 acts by James Elroy Flecker
Music by FD

Date: late 1920—summer 1921; additions, late 1923.

The original music provided by FD included preludes to all 5 acts as well as a number of incidental pieces. When the work was first staged in London, in the production by Basil Dean, not only were several of the numbers modified or extended at his request, but extra interludes were also called for, to cover the scene changes. *I understand now that there was too little music before I had written the additions* (FD to Percy Grainger, 29 September 1923).

As FD composed the bulk of the music before the play was published, he worked to a typescript 'in 5 books', listed on the 1935/2 list and also the 1952 one. This may still survive; and if so, it would be interesting to learn if it is a copy of the 'Leysin version' of the play, and if it has the same alterations as the author made in the copy thereof, now in the Bodleian Library, which became the text for the first publication of 1922.

To clarify the relation between the scenes of the originally-published play and Dean's acting edition, likewise between the original musical score and the 'new and complete edition', a concordance is drawn up on the following pages. It should be noted that there are also very considerable changes in the text between Flecker's play as originally written; as later revised; as published in 1922; and Dean's acting edition, details of which are outside the scope of the present work (cf. Sherwood op. cit. inf.).

Orchestra: 1 (also Picc). 1. CA. 1. 1—2. 1. 1.1—Timp. Xyl. Cym. Tambno. Camel Bells. Pavillon Chinois (on the stage) [in later version replaced by Cym. *tr.*]; in later version, also Side Drum, Wood Blocks & Trgl. in added 'General Dance'; Tamtam [not in later version]—Pianoforte (behind the scenes) [not in later version]—Harp—Strings (6 Vl. 2 Va. 2 Vc. CB).

Voices: Chorus (S.A.T.B)
Solo Tenor in [Serenade] (first version only)
                Voice from the Minaret
                [The cry of the Watchman] (later version only)
Solo Baritone (Chief of the Beggars)

HASSAN: Concordance of different versions

First edition, publ. Heinemann 1922 (using Flecker's first revision, i.e. the 'Leysin version' revised) (v. Sherwood, op. cit, 211)	*Basil Dean's acting edition* as published 1957 (Heinemann; The Drama Library); including 'all the author's last-minute cuts and alterations' (v. p. xviii of this edition)
Act I Scene 1	Act I Scene 1
Scene 2	Scene 2
Act II Scene 1	Scene 3
Scene 2	Scene 4
Act III Scene 1	Act II Scene 1
Scene 2	
Scene 3	Scene 2
Act IV Scene 1	Act III Scene 1
Scene 2	Scene 2
Act V Scene 1	Scene 3
Scene 2	Scene 4

Original Score (FD 1920)	New and Complete Edition (FD 1920–1923) (Neue vollständige Ausgabe)
Introduction	Introduction
	Act I: Interlude between Scenes 1 and 2
Act I, Scene 2: music, including Serenade (not so entitled) for Tenor and piano (off stage)	Act I, Scene 2: music, including Serenade (thus titled) for orchestra
	Chorus (behind the scenes)
Prelude to Act II	Prelude to Act II
Fanfare	Fanfare preceding the Ballet
Chorus (without words and unaccompanied)	
	Ballet:
Choruses of beggars & women	1. Dance of the Beggars
Divertissement	2. Chorus of Women ⎫ (extended)
	3. Divertissement ⎭
	4. General Dance
'A paradox in Paradise'	Chorus of Beggars and Dancing girls
Act II, Scene 2, music	Act II, Scene 2, music
	Music accompanying Ishak's poem
Prelude to Act III (with women's voices)	Prelude to Act III (with women's voices)
Curtain music	Act III. Interlude between Scenes 1 and 2 (= repeat of Serenade, differently scored)
Scene 2. Chorus of Soldiers	Act III. Scene 2. Chorus of Soldiers (extended)
Fanfares; Entry of the Caliph.	Fanfares; Entry of the Caliph; Fanfares
Prelude to Act IV	Prelude to Act IV
	Act IV. Interlude between Scenes 1 and 2
Prelude to Act V (with women's voices)	Prelude to Act V (with women's voices)
The song of the Muezzin at sunset	The song of the Muezzin at sunset
The Procession of Protracted Death	The Procession of Protracted Death
Prelude to the last scene [orig. 'The Ghost of the Artist of the Fountain rises from the Fountain itself'.]	Prelude to the last scene
	Closing Scene (Tenor solo) [the Song of the Watchman]
Male chorus	Mixed chorus (much extended)

MS: (*a*) Original full score, partly pencil in Delius's autograph (inked over in mauve by another hand), partly in the hand of Philip Heseltine, Boosey & Hawkes archives, n.d., pp. 127. Jelka Delius has added the German translation of words, stage directions and tempo indications throughout; she has also often written the clefs etc. for those pages inked in in mauve ink. This score establishes the original conception of the musical portion of the work.
Facsimile of an excerpt, DLP 80.

(*b*). Additions to the music, full score in the hand of Jelka Delius (late 1923), '52 big pages' (v. letter from JD to Marie Clews, 4 August 1923, quoted in TB 192). At present these sheets remain unlocated.

(*c*). Full score (pp. 239 in all) and performing material of the complete work, revised version as performed at His Majesty's Theatre, London, in 1923 (v. inf.). In copyists' hands; some pasted-in printed insertions (from vocal score); cues and markings, some in the hand of Percy E. Fletcher; also some blue pencilling (e.g. in the Intermezzo and Serenade) probably in Beecham's hand. Formerly the property of Basil Dean, all this material was acquired from him by Boosey & Hawkes in July 1970.

(*d*). Full score of the complete work, in professional copyists' hands, Boosey & Hawkes archives, pp. 171 in all. Beecham's blue pencilling. This score appears to have been at first a copyist's copy of the original score (a) above, Ger. text with Eng. trans. below. The extra pages for the additions and alterations, in a different and neater hand, and with Eng. text above Ger., were evidently pasted in later. In this score, no specific instrument is named for the Serenade, but 'cello' is pencilled over the melody line. In the last scene, at the closing chorus, 'sopr. and contr.' is likewise pencilled on the male voice staves.

(*e*). Rough sketches, chiefly in pencil; some in Delius's hand and some in Jelka Delius's, DT 39 ff 111–14 (RL 149).
Facsimile of an excerpt, DLP 80.

(*f*). Music to Act I scene 2 (original version), pencil draft, partly in Delius's hand, partly in Jelka Delius's, BL Add. MS 50497, pp. 4.

(*g*). 'Sketches for "Dance" from "Hassan" late July, 1923, Lesjaskog', in the hand of Percy Grainger, BL Add. MS 50879, ff 16–18a. This is the short-score draft of the General Dance added in the later version, and corresponds to pp. 28 1. 3 (at 'Allegro')—33 of the revised printed vocal score. See Grainger to Eric Fenby, 6 December 1936 (quoted in RL 168); also FD to Grainger, 29 September 1923: Our *ballet piece was a* great success *and brought just a vigorous contrast to the rest.*

Publication: 1923, HASSAN or The Golden Journey to Samarkand. Piano score arranged by Philip Heseltine (Deutscher Text der Gesänge von R. St. Hoffmann), Universal Edition 6966, Eng. Ger., pp. 40. Date after Delius's name: (1920).

1924(?), HASSAN [*tout simple*]. ditto, 'New and complete edition (Neue vollständige Ausgabe)', Universal Edition 6966, Eng. Ger., pp. 67. Date after Delius's name: (1920–1923).

1939, the work having passed to Boosey & Hawkes Ltd., an unaltered reprint of the 'New and complete edition' (but not so styled) was issued in 1965 as Boosey & Hawkes 18680.

The full score in the Composer's orchestration remains unpublished, with the exception of the following two excerpts:

1940, *Intermezzo* [i.e. from Act I, between scenes 1 and 2] and *Serenade*, edited by Sir Thomas Beecham, Boosey & Hawkes 8372, full score, and later (1941–2) included in HPS 23, 8658, miniature score.

Performance: 1 June 1923 et seq., Darmstadt. (Ger. trans. of the play by Ernst Freissler). This performance utilized the original version of the music, less some cuts, and the unrevised 'Leysin version' of the play (v. Sherwood, op. cit. p. 224).

20 September 1923, London, His Majesty's Theatre, produced by Basil Dean (with the music in the revised version). Cond: Eugène Goossens for the opening night; subsequently Percy E. Fletcher.

Arrangements: *Serenade:*
1923, for solo piano (from Philip Heseltine's piano score, but re-engraved), Universal Edition 10517. 1939, transferred to Boosey & Hawkes and later reprinted as 15170, pp. 3.

1923, for violin and piano, arranged by Lionel Tertis, Universal Edition 7628. 1939, transferred to Boosey & Hawkes and later reprinted as 15171, pp. 3, 1.

1931, for cello and piano, arranged by Eric Fenby, Universal Edition 5605, 5605b. 1939, transferred to Boosey & Hawkes and later reprinted as 15317, pp. 6, 1.

1934, for organ, arranged by Eric Fenby, Universal Edition 10622. Transferred to Boosey & Hawkes and later reprinted as 16630, pp. 3.

1934, for viola and piano, arranged by Lionel Tertis, Universal Edition 10623. Transferred to Boosey & Hawkes and later reprinted as 16888, pp. 3, 1.

?1929, *Suite*, arranged by Eric Fenby for full orchestra. (2 (Picc). 1. CA. 2. 2—4. 2. 3. 1—Timp. Cym. T Mil. Trgl. Wood Block. Camel Bells. Xyl—Harp—Strings), MS Boosey & Hawkes, unpubl.
This originally consisted of the following movements:
(i) Prelude to Act I.
(ii) Prelude to Act II and Ballet.
(iii) Serenade (for solo cello, accomp. by strings, first *pizz.* then *arco*, and woodwind).
(iv) Procession of Protracted Death.
(v) Desert Scene (= p. 56 of revised piano score onwards).
Subsequently the preludes to Acts I and II were removed, and later the whole sequence was reversed thus: Desert Scene—Procession—Serenade—Ballet. (Broadcast 1 August 1933, BBC orchestra, cond. Victor Hely-Hutchinson).

See also Jelka Delius to Norman O'Neill, 24 April 1929: 'Fred has just made a glorious orchestral suite with chorus of the *Hassan* music, with the aid of Eric Fenby'. (Quoted in Derek Hudson, *Norman O'Neill*, p. 73); but see also EF 50, 57 and RL 168.
Note: Sir Thomas Beecham, in his concert performances of extracts from the work—with or without voices—used the original orchestration.

Notes: TB 189, 192; EF 44, 50, 57; RL 167–8.

Philip Heseltine: *Hassan*. Mr. Delius's Music, review in the *Daily Telegraph*, 29 September 1923.

See also John Sherwood, *No Golden Journey*, Heinemann (London, 1973), pp. 201–11; 223–5.

The original (copyist's) MS orchestral material of the original version (used at Darmstadt) with Jelka Delius's Ger. trans. of the Eng. directions is now in the Boosey & Hawkes Opera Library; Universal Edition labels on first pages, at foot.

Play:

James Elroy Flecker (1884–1915): The Story of Hassan of Bagdad and how he came to make the Golden Journey to Samarkand (first edition, 1922; and see Sherwood loc. cit.).

II Works for voices and orchestra:

II/1 MITTERNACHTSLIED ZARATHUSTRAS
aus Also sprach Zarathustra
von Friedrich Nietzsche
für Baritone Solo, Männerchor & Orchester (B major)

Date: 1898, Grez-sur-Loing (MS). Signature *Frederick Delius* evidently altered from 'Fritz' at a later date.

Dedication: 'Meinem Freunde Arthur Krönig gewidmet'.

Orchestra: 3. 3. CA. 3. BsCl. 3. Contra—4. 3. 3 (Tenors). 1—Timp. Cym. 'Ein tiefe E♭ Glocke oder ein sehr tiefes Tam-Tam'—2 Harps—Strings.

MS: Autograph full score, DT 14 ff 1—19 (RL 66–7) pp. 33, dated. Text in Ger. only.
Facsimile of part of a page in DLP 57.

Publication: This work is essentially part II/6 (without the closing section) of *A Mass of Life*, q.v. for publication; and it corresponds with pp. 174–194 of the full score thereof except that men's voices only are called for (the women's voices being pencilled into the MS in preparation for the later layout). A similar ending to that of the last 7 bars of the Mass follows in conclusion (RL 67 refers).

Performance: 30 May 1899, London, St. James's Hall, Douglas Powell, cond. Alfred Hertz.

Words: Fr. Nietzsche, *Also sprach Zarathustra*, IV, 'Das trunkne Lied', 2 (end), 3, 12. Many performances of this work (though not the first one) programmed it under the title of 'Das trunkene Lied' or 'Das Nachtlied Zarathustras'.

Notes: PW 44–5 (56–9); TB 95–6, 100, 124.
The basically unaltered transfer of this score to the *Mass* of 1904–5 explains the use, in the corresponding section of the latter, of different keys for the brass instruments from those used in the rest of that work. Richard Strauss's tone-poem 'Also sprach Zarathustra' dates from 1896; Gustav Mahler's setting of section 12 only of 'Das trunkene Lied' forms the fourth movement of his Third Symphony (1895–6).

II/2 **APPALACHIA**
Variationen über ein altes Sklavenlied
mit Schlusschor für grosses Orchester

Date: 1902 (PW). Chop (Neue Musikzeitung XXXI, 1910, p. 313) 1903.

Dedication: 'Julius Buths gewidmet'.

Orchestra: 3 (also 3 picc). 3. CA. 2. E flat Cl. BsCl. 3. Contra—6. 3. 3.* 1
—Timp. BD. Cym. Trgl. Tamt. Side Dr.—2 Harps—Strings: 16. 16. 12.
12. 10.
* Trb. tenors, according to letters FD to Bantock, 26 February, 16
March 1908.

Chorus: Up to 8 parts; baritone solo sings in the chorus.

MS: Autograph full score, originally with Harmonie-Verlag (according to
the contract), now lost. Facsimile of bars 283–289 in Chop, 32.

Publication: 1906, Verlag Harmonie, Berlin (London: Breitkopf & Härtel),
full score, 170 (lithographed) pp. 100, Ger. and Eng.

1907, ditto, vocal score (Klavierauszug) by Otto Singer, 175 (Stich und
Druck von C. G. Röder, GmbH, Leipzig), pp. 30, Ger. and Eng.

1921, Transferred to Universal Edition catalogues, full score 3897, vocal
score 3900. (Chorus parts 3899 a–d).

1927, Engraved for miniature score, UE 7015 and W. Phil. V. 209, pp.
148, with portrait, 1914 (F. Müller, München, head & shoulders, $\frac{3}{4}$ left)
and preface signed 'Dr. A. P.' Some minor alterations included.

1939, the work having passed to Boosey & Hawkes, London, the
miniature score was reprinted, without portrait or preface, to their
number 8742, being issued as HPS 41 during the 'forties. Analysis, signed
E(rnst) R(oth), loosely inserted.

1951, Re-engraved for 'Complete Works. Revised and Edited by Sir
Thomas Beecham, Bart.', Boosey & Hawkes, full score 8911, pp. 117.

1969, Chorus parts reprinted, Boosey & Hawkes 19649 a–d. HPS 41
reissued by Boosey & Hawkes, but now reduced from Beecham edition,
8911, with a few corrections.

Performance: 15 October 1904, Elberfeld, Stadthalle, Elberfelder
Konzertgesellschaft, Elberfelder Gesangverein, cond. Hans Haym.

13 June 1905, Düsseldorf, cond. Julius Buths.

5 February 1906, Berlin, Philharmonic Orchestra, cond. Oskar Fried.

22 November 1907, London, Queen's Hall, New Symphony Orchestra,
Sunday League choir, cond. Fritz Cassirer.

2 April 1908, Hanley, Victoria Hall, Hallé Orchestra, N. Staffordshire
District Choral Society, cond. F. Delius.

Arrangements: March 1942, reduced score by Edward J. Dent (2. 2. 2. 2—4. 2(3). 3. 1—Timp. Perc.—Harp—Strings) MS, DT 47 (RL 159), pp. 130; material, Boosey & Hawkes.

1970, 'Appalachia for 4-part mixed chorus and piano'. Transcribed by Benjamin Suchoff, pp. 9. Sam Fox Publishing Company Inc., New York.

1975, Reduction in choral score, for use with Dent's reduced orchestration, by Eric Fenby. Boosey & Hawkes Hire Library.

Notes: PW 124–6 (113–4); CD 158–161; MC 64; TB 146–7, 149; Nettel 99. Chop 20 lists the work as item 10. See also: Ernest Newman, review in *Birmingham Daily Post*, 25 November 1907.

The original Harmonie full and vocal scores carried the following note: *'Appalachia is the old Indian name for North America. The composition mirrors the moods of tropical nature in the great swamps bordering on the Mississippi River, which is so intimately associated with the life of the old negro slave population. Longing melancholy, an intense love of Nature, childlike humour and an innate delight in singing and dancing are still the most characteristic qualities of this race.'*
This note was not reprinted in the later editions of the score. The programme of the 1905 performance (at the Lower Rhine Festival, Düsseldorf) gave the title as follows:
'Appalachia (Dixieland) (Eindrücke aus dem Süden). Introduktion, Thema mit Variationen und Finale. Symphonische Dichtung für grosses Orchester, Baritone-Solo und Chor'.

The chorus parts mark an 8-bar Vi-de immediately preceding the entry of the baritone solo, at cue Dd.

For the earlier orchestral work of the same title, partly utilizing the same thematic material, see p. 133.

Oskar Fried to FD:
4 January 1906: 'Appalachia is damned difficult'.
5 January 1906: 'Come to Berlin at once. The orchestral parts of Appalachia are in an incredible state . . . No expression marks or else they are defective—whether it should be the large flute or the piccolo is not clear, with two bassoons one never knows whether one is in the tenor or the bass clef . . .'

II/3 **IM MEERESTREIBEN**
Sea Drift
Text von Walt Whitman
für Bariton Solo, gemischten Chor und grosses Orchester
[Symphonic Poem]—(in advert. on Harmonie back covers)

Date: 1903 (PW); 1904 according to vocal score and Max Chop.

Dedication: 'Max Schillings gewidmet'.

Orchestra: 3. 3. CA. 3. BsCl. 3. Contra—6. 3. 3. 1—Timp. BD.—2 Harps—
Strings.

Chorus: up to 8 parts.

MS: Autograph full score, originally with Harmonie-Verlag (according to
the contract), now lost. Facsimile of bars 436, 437–443 in Chop, p. 56,
reproduced in DLP 55. This clearly shows the Eng. words in FD's hand,
with Ger. trans. below in Jelka Delius's hand. (FD to Ernest Newman,
19 August 1929, states: *I composed 'Sea Drift' in English and could not
have done otherwise, as the lovely poem inspired my music.* See also
notes inf.)

Publication: 1906, Verlag Harmonie, Berlin, full score (no plate no.),
lithographed, pp. 67, Ger. (by Jelka Rosen) and Eng. Front cover
bilingual, Ger. above and larger than Eng. (FD altered his copy to Eng.
above Ger.!)

Note: Delius's own copy of the full score, now in the DT archive, has
many corrections to notes, altered or added dynamics, and some
additions to the orchestration, e.g. the woodwind figuration strengthened
and doubled between cues 7 and 8.

1906, ditto, vocal score by Siegfried Fall, 168 (Stich u. Druck von C. G.
Röder GmbH Leipzig), pp. 39, Ger. and Eng. Two separate
(?simultaneous) issues of the vocal score appeared, one with Ger.
wording only on the cover and one with Eng. only. See DLP 54.

1921, Transferred to Universal Edition catalogues, full score 3893, vocal
score 3896, small vocal score (used as choral score) 3896a.

1928, Engraved for miniature score, UE 8886 and W. Phil. V. 215, pp. 96,
with portrait 1914 (F. Müller, München, ½ length, left profile) and words
printed separately at front. All the alterations mentioned above are taken
in to this edition.

1939, the work having passed to Boosey & Hawkes, the miniature score
was reprinted, without the portrait, to their number 8743; being issued as
HPS 43 during the 'forties. Analysis (unsigned) loosely inserted.

1951, Re-engraved for 'Complete Works. Revised and Edited by Sir
Thomas Beecham, Bart.' Boosey & Hawkes, full score 8915, pp. 83.
Vocal score reissued 'Revised by Sir Thomas Beecham, Bart.' Boosey &
Hawkes 18102.

HPS 43 in hand (1977) for reissue, reduced from the Beecham edition
8915, with a few corrections, as a study score.

Performance: 24 May 1906, Essen, Tonkünstlerfest, Allgemeine Deutsche Musikverein, Josef Loritz, cond. Georg Witte.

1/2 March 1907, Basle, cond. Hermann Suter.

7 October 1908, Sheffield, Queen's Hall Orchestra, Sheffield Festival Chorus, Frederick Austin, cond. Henry J. Wood.

Words: Walt Whitman (1819–92): *Leaves of Grass*, Sea-Drift, 'Out of the Cradle Endlessly Rocking', lines 23–129, with omissions of lines 47–8 and 86–92 inclusive.

Notes: PW 103–5 (99–100); TB 122–3, 135, 154; Nettel 101–2. Chop 20 lists the work as item 11. See also: Ernest Newman, review in *Birmingham Daily Post*, 8 October 1908.

A copy of the Harmonie printed full score bearing Sir Thos. Beecham's performance markings is also in the DT Archive.

Georg Witte to FD, April 1906: 'I should like . . . to ask whether you will permit me to "touch up" the choral parts a little in the interests of more comfortable singing and a better rendering of the German text'. For FD's reaction, see TB 135 and EF 204.

Philip Heseltine, writing in 1915 (Musical Times, March 1915, p. 137) states: 'It is noteworthy that he has had to have the English words to which he has set music translated into German in order to get a hearing'.

II/4 **EINE MESSE DES LEBENS**
A MASS OF LIFE
Worte aus 'Also sprach Zarathustra' von Friedrich Nietzsche
zusammengestellt von Fritz Cassirer,
Für Sopran, Alt, Tenor, Bariton [soli], gemischten [Doppel] Chor und
grosses Orchester.

Erster Teil:
1. Animato (Double chorus)
2. Animoso ('Recitative' in full score) (Baritone solo)
3. Andante tranquillo con dolcezza (Tutti)
4. Agitato ma moderato (Baritone & chorus)
5. Andante molto tranquillo ('Adagio' in full score) (Baritone & chorus)

Zweiter Teil:
Auf den Bergen [Fl, 3 Horns, Timp. & Strings] (untitled in full score and
Harmonie vocal score).
1. Con elevazione e vigore (Double chorus and soli except baritone)
2. Andante (Baritone solo)
3. Lento (in full score 'molto') (Baritone and women's voices)
4. Lento (in vocal score 'molto') (Tutti)
5. Allegro ma non troppo, con gravità (Baritone and chorus)
6. Largo con solennità (Baritone solo, later tutti)

Date: 1904–5. (Part II/6, 1898).

Dedication: 'Meinem Freunde Fritz Cassirer gewidmet'. Part II/6 still
carries the original dedication to Arthur Krönig, v. supra,
Mitternachtslied.

Orchestra: 3 (alt. Picc). 3 (incl. CA). BsOb. 3. BsCl. 3. Contra—6. 4. 3
(Tenors). 1—Timp. BD. Side Dr. Cym. Trgl. Castanets. Glockenspiel.
Tamt. 2 Bells—2 Harps—Strings: 16. 16. 12. 12. 12.

MS: (*a*). Autograph full score, ?originally with Harmonie-Verlag
(according to contract), now lost.

(*b*). A 2-volume MS (?copy) appears on the 1935/1 list as item 29: 'Ein
Messe des Lehens [sic] 1905 (2 books)', also as items 7–8 on the 1952 list.
This is presumably the score also shown on the Beecham Libr. list.

(*c*). Copyist's MS, Universal Edition Archiv, Vienna (letter to the present
writer dated 13 July 1973 from Stefan Harpner refers).

Publication: 1907, Verlag Harmonie, Berlin, full score (2 volumes), 222,
lithographed (Autographie u. Druck von C. G. Röder GmbH Leipzig),
pp. 203, Ger. and Eng. (the latter by John Bernhoff). As this publication,
printed in all probability from the original autograph, predates the first
performance, a large number of minor errors were included.

1907, ditto, vocal score by Otto Singer, 183, engraved (presumably by
C. G. Röder) pp. 210, Ger. and Eng. See DLP 56.

1921, Transferred to Universal Edition catalogues, full score 3904–5,
vocal score 3908, choral score 3908a, pp. 74 (extract from vocal score).
Some minor corrections, and some alterations, were made in the later
UE-printed vocal score, e.g. the Baritone solo at cue 40 on p. 86 was

omitted; accidentals were supplied to the chord on p. 151 bar 6; and chorus parts were added on p. 163, last 2 bars.

—Tonic sol-fa edition, UE 10344, pp. 41.

1969, Choral score reprinted by Boosey & Hawkes, 19853 ('Copyright 1924 by Universal Edition').

1972, having been transferred to Boosey & Hawkes in 1952, a study score (HPS 879) was now issued. 'This edition is a reprint in reduced format of the full score originally published in 1907 in two volumes by Harmonie-Verlag, Berlin (no. 222)'. Inserted was an errata slip prepared by R. Threlfall giving corrections based on a marked copy of the full score given to the DT by Eric Fenby, into which most had been entered by Henry Gibson from Sir Thomas Beecham's copy. A revised errata slip dated 10/73 was issued with the reprint in 1975.

Note: Analysis by Hans Haym, and complete book of words, publ. Universal Edition 3913 n.d. (Eng. trans. UE 8256, 1925).

Performance: 4 June 1908, Munich, Tonkünstlerfest; M. van Lammen, Olga von Welden, Benno Hebert, Rudolf Gmür, Konzertgesellschaft für Chorgesang, Münchener Hofkapelle, cond. Ludwig Hess. [Part I/2 and Part II (with cuts in II/3 and II/5) only].

7 June 1909, London, Queen's Hall; Gleeson White, M. G. Grainger-Kerr, Webster Millar, Charles Clark (?Stanley Adams), North Staffordshire District Choral Society, Beecham Orchestra, cond. Thomas Beecham.

11 December 1909, Elberfeld, Stadthalle; Emma Tester, Meta Diestel, Matthäus Römer, Charles Clark, Elberfelder Gesangverein, cond. Hans Haym.

Words: Friedrich [Wilhelm] Nietzsche (1844–1900): 'Also sprach Zarathustra' (1883–4).

(M. of L.) (A.s.Z.)

I, 1	III, Von alten und neuen Tafeln, 30 (condensed)
2	IV, Von höheren Menschen, 17, 18, 19, 20 (parts)
3	III, Das andere Tanzlied, 1, 2 (part) 3; the Baritone solo from IV, Das Eselsfest, 3 (part)
4	IV, Das trunkne Lied, 4
5	II, Das Nachtlied (excerpts)
II, 1	IV, Das Zeichen (end) and III, Von alten und neuen Tafeln, 28, 29 (excerpts); soli from II, Vom Gesindel (excerpts)
2	IV, Das trunkne Lied, 6
3	II, Das Tanzlied (excerpts)
4	IV, Mittags (excerpts)
5	IV, Das trunkne Lied, 8 (condensed)
6	IV, Das trunkne Lied, 2 (end), 3, 12, 11 (condensed)

Notes: PW 105–114 (100–106); TB 132–3; Nettel 102–6. Chop, p. 20, lists the work as item 12.

Another English translation was made for Beecham by William Wallace, TB chap. 22; and a paraphrase by 'Peter Warlock' appeared in the programme of the Delius Festival performance on 1 November 1929.

In his public performances, certainly from 1929 on, Beecham altered the order of the movements as follows: After part I he continued with II/1 and II/4, after which came the interval. As the second part then came II/2, 3, 5 & 6. Some other conductors have followed this on occasion, or at least have placed the interval after II/1 instead of before it (as Sir Malcolm Sargent did). It must be admitted that any of these expedients upsets the double-arch form of the work, as so clearly described by Deryck Cooke (see programme notes, Royal Philharmonic Society, Royal Albert Hall 3 November 1964), although doubtless Beecham had the composer's sanction for the change.

Sir Malcolm Sargent's performing material, now in the Boosey Hire Library, is used by the BBC. This involves not only reduction to treble woodwind and 4 horns, but occasional strengthening of the basses with Tuba or Double bass; also added brass to support the choir at several points (e.g. Trumpets in triple-tonguing at the very start, on F).

The two themes of the opening section of *Over the hills and far away* are woven into the texture of II/1 between cues 61 and 64.

II/5 SONGS OF SUNSET
Sonnenuntergangs-Lieder
(Poems by Ernest Dowson)
(Deutsche Übertragung von Jelka Rosen)
For Soprano and Baritone Solo, mixed chorus and Orchestra

Date: 1906–1908 according to published full score. A letter from FD to Bantock, 19 September 1907, states: *I have just finished a cyclus of songs by Ernest Dowson.*

Dedication: 'Dem Elberfelder Gesangverein gewidmet'.

Orchestra: 3. 1. CA. BsOb. 3. 3. Sarrus (Contra)—4. 2. 3 (Tenors). 1 —Timp. Trgl. BD.—Harp—Strings: 14. 14. 12. 10. 8.

Chorus: 4-part.

MS: (*a*). Autograph full score, originally with Leuckart (according to contract), now lost.

(*b*). A MS with the earlier title *Songs of Twilight and Sadness* appears as item 5 on the 1935/2 list, and 'Sketches: Songs of Twilight' appears as part of item 38 on the 1952 list. A MS of 'They are not long, the weeping & the laughter' is included in the Beecham Libr. list.

(*c*). A MS sheet giving corrections required in the original printed editions of both full and vocal scores is now to be found in DT 39 f 115 (RL 149).

Publication: 1911, F. E. C. Leuckart, Leipzig, full score 6736, pp. 51, Ger. and Eng. text (the former by Jelka Rosen).
Note: a set of plate-pulls of this score, with some corrections and many performance marks by Sir Thos. Beecham, is now in the DT Archive.

1911, ditto, vocal score (by Dagmar Juhl, but not so attributed, v. letters 29 August 1912 FD to G. Tischer: *Dagmar Juhl did . . . Songs of Sunset*), 6738, pp. 39, Ger. and Eng. Separate chorus parts 6739.

1921, Transferred to Universal Edition catalogues, full score handled as 6915, parts 6916, chorus parts 6917 a–d, vocal score 6918.

1975, Study score, also numbered 6915, issued by Universal together with a reprint of the vocal score (6918); both incorporating the corrections mentioned above (from DT 39 f 115) and a few further ones.
Note: in the USA this work is handled by Boosey & Hawkes Inc.

Performance: 16 June 1911, London, Queen's Hall; Julia Culp, Thorpe Bates, Edward Mason choir, Beecham orchestra, cond. Thomas Beecham.

Words: Ernest Dowson (1867–1900):

'A song of the setting sun' (chorus) — *Moritura* (from *Decorations*, posth., omitting the third of the 4 verses)

'Cease smiling, Dear!' (soli) — fr. *Verses*, 1896, omitting verses 2 & 4 of the 8 verses

'Pale amber sunlight falls' (chorus) — *Autumnal* (from *Verses*, omitting the last of the 4 stanzas)

'Exceeding sorrow' (soprano)	*O Mors! Quam amara est memoria tua* *homini pacem habenti in substantiis tuis* (*Verses*, 4 stanzas complete)
'By the sad waters of separation' (baritone)	*Exile* (*Verses*, 5 stanzas complete; 'her' for 'your' in last line of v. 3)
'See how the trees . . .' (soli and chorus)	*In Spring* (*Decorations*, 2 verses complete)
'I was not sorrowful' (baritone)	*Spleen* (*Verses*, 7 couplets complete)
'They are not long' (soli and chorus)	*Vitae summa brevis spem nos vetat* *incohare longam* [Horace, Odes I, iv, 15] (*Verses*, 2 stanzas complete)

Notes: PW 120–3 (111–2); TB 167.

In 1913, Arnold Schönberg completed a setting of Dowson's *Seraphita*
with orchestral accompaniment, published as his op. 22 no. 4.

II/6 THE SONG OF THE HIGH HILLS
(Das Lied von den hohen Bergen)
(mit Schlusschor)—[F. E. C. Leuckart edn. only]
For orchestra and wordless chorus

Date: 1911 on published score.

Dedication: none.

Orchestra: 3 (incl. Picc). 2. CA. 3. BsCl. 3. Sarrus (Contra)—6. 3. 3
(Tenors). 1—Timp (3 players). BD. Cym. Glockenspiel—Celesta. 2
Harps—Strings: 16. 16. 12. 12. 10.

Chorus: up to 8 parts; Soprano and Tenor soli in the chorus. 'Der Chor
muss auf dem Vokal gesungen werden, der den Ausdruck der Musik am
besten wiedergibt'.

MS: (*a*). Autograph full score, presumably originally with Leuckart, now
lost.

(*b*). Sketches, DT 39 ff 70–76 (RL 143–4). A portion of these sketches
headed *Symphonie*.

(*c*). Further sketches, Grainger Museum, Melbourne, Australia (see
SM7, pp. 72, 76).

Publication: [1915] (no date but BL cat. thus) F. E. C. Leuckart, Leipzig,
full score 7254, pp. 50.

1921, Transferred to Universal Edition, Vienna, and handled by them to
no. 6912; also choral score (Chorparticell), 6899, pp. 16 ('copyright 1919
by F. E. C. Leuckart, Leipzig').

1923, Universal Edition, study score, 7016 (a photographic reduction of
the above).

1964, Universal Edition, miniature score, 13875 (an even smaller
reduction of the original).

Performance: 26 February 1920, London, Queen's Hall, Royal
Philharmonic Society, Philharmonic Choir, cond. Albert Coates.

Arrangements: 1921, for piano solo by Philip Heseltine. MS, DT 22 ff 1–15
(RL 83; and plate 22, facsimile of first page), pp. 27, unpubl. Gray 243
(letter from Philip Heseltine to Gray 19 November 1921 refers).
Heseltine is known to have made an earlier piano/vocal score of the work
(v. Copley, op. cit.) but whether this is the basis of the printed
'Chorparticell', UE 6899, is uncertain as the latter publication makes no
such acknowledgment.

1923, for two pianos by Percy Grainger. A MS DT 22, ff 16–30 (RL 83)
dated. Facsimile of a page, GC 71. Unpublished. Another MS, Grainger
Museum, Melbourne; another one, Percy Grainger Library Society,
White Plains, New York.

1942(?), Reduced score by Edward J. Dent. MS untraced (not with UE
London on enquiry in 1969).

Notes: PW 126–7 (114–5); TB 168.

A copy of the printed full score bearing Sir Thomas Beecham's markings
is now in the DT Archive.

II/7 AN ARABESQUE—Eine Arabeske
(Jens P. Jacobsen)
(Deutsche Übertragung von Jelka-Rosen)
For Baritone solo, mixed chorus and orchestra

Date: Autumn 1911 on MS, 1911 on printed scores. Beecham (TB 172, MC 142) refers to some partial rewriting in 1915.

Dedication: 'Halfdan Jebe gewidmet'.

Orchestra: 3. 2. CA. BsOb. 3. BsCl. 3. Sarrus—4. 3. 3 (Tenors). 1—Timp. Trgl. Xyl. Tambno.—Celesta, Harp—Strings.

Chorus: 4-part, with some divisions.

MS: Autograph full score, partly ink over pencil, *An Arabesk*, Universal Edition Archiv, on loan to the British Library, Loan 54/3, dated Autumn 1911, pp. 36. Titlepage in Eng. and Ger., the words set are in German only: a note by the publisher (on the titlepage) instructs the engraver to 'leave space under the text for the translation'. Tempo indications appear in Eng. and Ger. There are some corrections to accidentals, etc. in blue and red pencil (?by the publisher's reader). The principal signs in this MS of the rewriting mentioned by Beecham as taking place while FD was his guest at Grove Mill House, Watford, in 1915, are as follows: The last bar of p. 23 is deleted (=third bar before cue 11). Page 24—an inserted leaf written on one side only—bears the seven 4/4 bars replacing this; pp. 25–36 being renumbered thus in ink over the original pencilled 24–35. The extensive changes in the baritone solo part, presumably to accommodate it to a bass-baritone, are also marked into this MS; further changes to adapt stresses and pitches to the later Eng. trans. result in an extraordinary crop of "double-stops" in places.

Publication: 1913, Universal Edition, Vienna, Chorus parts 5294 a–d, Ger. only.

1914, ditto. Vocal score by Heinrich Hartmann, 5295, pp. 23, Ger. only titlepage, text and tempo indications. (Deutsche Übertragung von Jelka-Rosen).

Note: if Beecham's date is correct for the reworking mentioned above, this vocal score may well not have been issued until 1915 or later, despite the copyright date of 1914 on p. 3 (unless earlier and revised states were issued, of which I have found no trace).

1920, ditto, full score, 5358, pp. 34, Ger. and Eng. titlepage, text and tempo indications ('Done into English by Ph. Heseltine' [in 1914]). *Note:* the orchestral parts (5359) are plate-pulls.

Performance: FD writes to Ernest Newman, 12 November 1913: *In 10 days I leave for Vienna to attend the first performance of a new work—'An Arabesk', Baritone solo, mixed chorus & orchestra.* A letter to Percy Grainger a few days later (16 Nov.) repeats this information and gives 26 November as the performance date. A few years later, however, FD writing to Grainger on 11 January, 23 July and 15 November 1916 includes the work among those never performed; again, on 16 January

1919 FD repeats that it is *still awaiting performance*. It appears, then, that the Vienna performance did not materialize.

28 May 1920, Newport, Central Hall: Percy Heming, Welsh Musical Festival Choral Society, London Symphony Orchestra, cond. Arthur E. Sims.

Words: Jens Peter Jacobsen (1847–1885)—*Digte:*
'En Arabesk' (1868?) ('Har du faret vild i dunkle Skove? Kender du Pan?').

Notes: TB 167–8; 188.

FD to Ernest Newman, 19 August 1929: *... in composing ... the 'Arabesk' ... I composed to german words.*

A copy of the printed full score marked by Sir Thomas Beecham is in the DT Archive.

II/8 REQUIEM
für Sopran und Bariton, Doppel-Chor und Orchester

1. Feierlich. Solemnly (Double chorus and baritone solo)
2. Mit Kraft und Inbrust. With vigor and fervor (ditto)
3. Moderato; 'à la grande Amoureuse' [in MS & chorus parts only] (Baritone solo and chorus)
4. Mit Nachdruck. With Energy (Soprano solo and chorus)
5. Sehr Langsam. Very slow (tutti)

Date: 1914 (on MS and published score).

Dedication: 'Dem Andenken aller jungen Künstler die im Kriege gefallen/ To the memory of all young Artists fallen in the War'.

Orchestra: 3 (also Picc). 2. CA. BsOb. 3. BsCl. 3. Contra (Sarrus)—6. 3. 3. 1 (Trombones Tenor in MS, 2 Ten 1 Bass in printed score)—Timp. BD. Cym. T Mil. Trgl. Glockenspiel—Celesta, Harp—Strings.

MS: (*a*). Autograph full score, partly ink over pencil, Universal Edition Archiv, on loan to the British Library, Loan 54/4, dated 1914, pp. 80. Ger. only, but Eng. trans. pencilled below.

(*b*). Sketches, DT 39 ff 77–82 (RL 144–5); facsimile of a page in DLP 72.

(*c*).Further sketches, Grainger Museum, Melbourne, Australia (v. SM7, p. 75).

(*d*). A MS libretto, in the hand of Jelka Delius, now DT Archive.

Publication: 1920, Universal Edition, Vienna, chorus parts 6593 a–d.

1921, ditto, vocal score (by Philip Heseltine, but not so attributed) 6592, pp. 55, Ger. and Eng. text; 'The English version by Philip Heseltine'.

1922, ditto, full score, 6594, pp. 55, Ger. and Eng. text.

1923(?), ditto, study score, 7019 [not seen].

1965, the work having passed to Boosey & Hawkes, London, a study score (HPS 775) was issued, 19386, as well as a choral score, 19436, pp. 31 in 1966.

Performance: 23 March 1922, London, Queen's Hall, Royal Philharmonic Society; Amy Evans, Norman Williams, Philharmonic Choir, cond. Albert Coates.

6 November 1950, New York, Carnegie Hall, National Orchestra Association, cond. Wm. Jonson.

9 November 1965, Liverpool, Philharmonic Hall, Royal Liverpool Philharmonic Orchestra; Heather Harper, Thomas Hemsley, cond. Charles Groves.

Words: According to the contract between Delius and Universal Edition, the author of the text was Heinrich Simon, but no such acknowledgment is made in either MS or printed copies. The words appear to borrow from both the Old Testament (Ecclesiastes) and Nietzsche.
FD to Ernest Newman, 2 May [1919]: *I wonder whether you would undertake the translation from the German of my 'Requiem'—It is written rather in the style of the old Testament & it is short.*

Notes: PW 114–120 (106–110); CD 195–6; TB 172–3.
A photo-copy of the printed full score, bearing Sir Thomas Beecham's markings, is now in the DT Archive.

II/9 **SONGS OF FAREWELL**
(Lieder des Abschieds)
Choral work for Double Chorus and Orchestra
Words by Walt Whitman; German words by Jelka Delius.

1. Quieto, molto tranquillo
2. Lento molto
3. Andante tranquillo
4. Maestoso
5. Moderato con moto

Date: 1930 (on final MS and printed scores).

Dedication: 'To my wife'.

Orchestra: 2. 2. CA. 2. BsCl. 3. Contra—4. 3. 3. 1—Timp.—Harp—Strings: 16. 16. 12. 10. 8 [in MS].

Chorus: 8-part.

MS: (*a*). Draft full score in Eric Fenby's hand of nos. 2–5 (no. 1 was destroyed), Grainger Museum, Melbourne, dated 1929–30, pp. 9–36 (v. SM7, 76).

(*b*). Fair copy, full score in Eric Fenby's hand, Boosey & Hawkes archives, dated 1930, pp. 36, Eng. & Ger. (the latter interlined in red ink). Facsimile of a page from (5), DLP 88.

(*c*). Vocal score by Eric Fenby and in his hand, Boosey & Hawkes archives, pp. 44, Eng.; Ger. words interlined in red by Jelka Delius.

Publication: 1931, Boosey & Hawkes, vocal score by Eric Fenby, 6975, pp. 39, Eng. & Ger.

1931, ditto, full score, 7014, pp. 36, Eng. and Ger.

1936, Full score of (2) printed in miniature in Appendix to EF, pp. [237–242].

Performance: 21/22 March 1932, London, Queen's Hall, Philharmonic Choir, London Symphony Orchestra, cond. Dr. Malcolm Sargent.

Words: Walt Whitman, *Leaves of Grass:*

1. Sands at Seventy: 'Memories' and 'Out of May's Shows Selected.'
2. Sands at Seventy: 'From Montauk Point'.
3. Passage to India: 9, lines 11–20.
4. Songs of Parting: 'Joy, Shipmate, Joy!'.
5. Songs of Parting: 'Now Finalè to the Shore'.

Notes: TB 208; EF 101–2, 114–16, 147–57.
According to Eric Fenby (loc. cit. 147) 'the orchestral introduction [to the second movement] already existed in short score'. See also Jelka Delius to Ernest Newman, 28 October 1930: 'This work was entirely sketched out in 1920 or 21, when he put it aside to do the Hassan music' This doubtless explains some very close resemblances to the latter, e.g.

Songs of Farewell	*Hassan*
1, 3 bars before cue 30	Prelude to Act 3
2, cue 70	Prelude to Act 5, last 6 bars.

II/10 **IDYLL**
('Once I passed thro' a populous City')
['Eine volkreiche Stadt durchwandert' ich einst']
For Soprano, Baritone and Orchestra
Words adapted from Walt Whitman by Robert Nichols
(Ger. by Jelka Delius)

Date: Preface to published vocal score signed by Robert Nichols and Eric
Fenby, September–October 1932.

Dedication: none.

Orchestra: 2. 2.CA. 2. 2—4. 2. 3. 1—Timp.—Harp—Strings.

MS: (a). Full score in Eric Fenby's hand, Boosey & Hawkes archives, dated
1901(!), pp. 38. Some blue-pencil performance directions in the hand of
Sir Thomas Beecham.

(b). A copy of the above in the hand of Harold Perry is also in the
Boosey archives.

(c). Vocal score by Eric Fenby and in his hand, Boosey & Hawkes
archives, pp. 24. Ger. words interlined in red by Jelka Delius.

(d). Vocal score, a copy of (c) above, in the hand of Harold Perry, lacking
the prelude, also in the Boosey archives, pp. 21.

(e). A photographic copy of the original full score, with some cuts blanked
out and performance markings by Sir Thomas Beecham, is now in DT 33
44–63 (RL 106).

Publication: 1933, Boosey & Hawkes, vocal score by Eric Fenby, 13824,
pp. 25, Eng. and Ger.

1976, ditto, study score 20256 (HPS 901), pp. 67, Eng. & Ger., with
preface by Eric Fenby ("Prelude and Idyll").

Performance: 3 October 1933, London, Queen's Hall (Promenade Concert),
Dora Labette, Roy Henderson, BBC Symphony Orchestra, cond. Sir
Henry J. Wood.

Words: Walt Whitman; *Leaves of Grass:*

The words were 'selected and adapted' by Robert Nichols from *Children
of Adam, Calamus, The Sleepers*, and *Songs of Parting*. A detailed
concordance of the resulting synthetic text with the original poems is
beyond the scope of the present work.

Notes: TB 207–8; EF 119–121.

The music of the *Idyll* is extracted from the opera *Margot la Rouge* of
1901–2. For detailed concordance of vocal scores of the two works, see
RL 166 (Appendix 2). Originally, the Idyll was to have commenced with
the music of Scene 1 of the opera, but after the first performance the
Prelude to the opera was used as an orchestral introduction to the *Idyll*,
and the opening 12 bars of Scene 1 were then cut.
It should be remarked that none of the alterations marked in the various
copies of *Margot la Rouge* examined (cf. entry relating, pp. 42–43) are
observed in the corresponding passages of *Idyll*.

III Works for solo voice and orchestra:

III/1 PAA VIDDERNE
Auf dem Hochgebirge
Gedicht von H. Ibsen
Melodrama von Fritz Delius

1. Allegro vivace	(A♭ major)
2. Andante tranquillo	(E minor)
3. Adagietto con voglia	(F major)
4. Grave	(D minor)
5. Lento, molto tranquillo	(E major)
6. Andante, con voglia, molto tranquillo	(D minor)
7. Allegro furioso	(C minor)
8. Comodo	(E minor)
9. Lento con molto espressione	(G minor, D major)

Date: 1888 (MS).

Dedication: 'Edvard Grieg gewidmet'.

Orchestra: Picc. 2. 2. CA. 2. 2—4. 2. 3 (Tenors). 1—Timp. BD. Cym. 2 Bells—Strings.

MS: Autograph full score DT 2 (RL 20–21), pp. 120, dated 1888. Text in Ger. only. Separate typescripts of text in Norwegian and English, DT 2a.

Publication: none. Facsimile of p. 65 of the MS, RL 20. A 13-bar excerpt (in piano arrangement), GC 39.

Performance: none as far as known.

Words: Henrik Ibsen (1828–1906): *Paa Vidderne* (1859–60); the complete poem in nine sections. (Ger. trans. by L. Passarge.)

Notes: TB 47–9.
The work was originally intended for Tenor voice (FD to Grieg, 20 June 1888). Later that summer FD wrote to Grieg: *Paa Vidderne I am revising completely . . . & indeed as a melodrama with orchestral accompaniment. It has not pleased me up to now.* Completed in this form by October, it was sent to Grieg, who acknowledged its receipt on 23 November. During subsequent correspondence concerning the viability of melodrama in general, and this specimen in particular, FD wrote: *I have written the whole thing so that I could write with ease a voice part for it.*
A phrase occurs in this work which is later used at the very end of the later eponymous orchestral overture of 1890–2, as also in *Over the hills and far away* of 1895–7. This phrase will be recognized in the horn parts of the last 2 bars of RL's plate 2 (RL 20).

III/2 SAKUNTALA
Gedicht von Holger Drachmann
für Tenor Stimme & Orchester von Fritz Delius

(G major; C–G)

Date: 1889 (MS).

Dedication: none.

Orchestra: 3. 2. CA. 2. BsCl. 2—4. 0. 0. 0—Timp.—2 Harps—Strings.

MS: Autograph full score DT 4 ff 1–14 (RL 27–29), pp. 25, dated 1889.
Text in German translation only. Separate Tenor voice part, DT 4 ff
15–16, Ger. only.

Publication: none. Facsimile of titlepage and first page of score, RL 27–8.

Performance: none as far as known; although the existence of the separate
voice part (with sundry pencillings thereon) points to the possibility of at
least a 'read-through'.

Words: Holger Drachmann (1846–1908): from *Songes*, 4 verses complete.
First appearing in 1876 in his novel *En Overkomplet*, Drachmann
reissued this, his most famous poem, in 1879 in the collection *Ranker og
Roser, en samling sange*. For this, as for other similar information on
Drachmann's works, I gratefully acknowledge the generous help of
Dr. John Bergsagel.
The Ger. trans. is by Edmund Lobedanz; from 'Ausgewählte Gedichte
von . . . anderen neueren nordischen Dichtern' (Leipzig, Wilhelm
Friedrich, Dichtungen des Auslandes, Band VII, 1881): Sakuntala (nach
H. D.) (A German translation by E. Lobedanz of the Sanskrit writer
Kālidāsa's 'Sakuntalā, or the fatal Ring: an Indian drama in 7 acts'
appeared first in 1854). (Sakuntala, Indisches Schauspiel nach Kalidasa).
Note: Delius's MS originally bore exactly this title, see RL 27 (plate 4),
29.

Note: Almost the first 'modern' orchestral song by a composer later to
become established. The composition (probably) and publication
(certainly) of Mahler's first orchestral songs postdate these early efforts
of Delius's; and Richard Strauss's first songs with orchestra, whether
original or arranged, date from 1896–7 (except for the 14-year old's
unpublished 'Der Spielmann und sein Kind' of 1878, obviously unknown
to Delius). Norman Del Mar, in his *Richard Strauss*, vol. iii, pp. 254–7,
has some well-considered words to say on the orchestral song and its
curious neglect in performance.

See also TB 54.

III/3 **MAUD**

[Five songs for tenor and orchestra with words by Tennyson]

[1.]	Birds in the high Hall-garden	(E major; B–G♯ (B))
[2.]	I was walking a mile	(C major; C–A)
[3.]	Go not happy day	(G major; B–B)
[4.]	Rivulet crossing my ground	(D minor—F major; F–G)
[5.]	Come into the Garden, Maud	(G major; C–G♯ (A♯))

Date: Fritz Delius 1891 (on MSS of three of the items).

Dedication: none.

Orchestra: (1). 3. 2. CA. 2. 2—4. 2. 0. 0—Timp.—Harp—Strings.
(2). 3. 2. CA. 2. 2—4. 0. 0. 0—Timp.—Harp—Strings.
(3). 3. 2. CA. 2. BsCl. 2—4. 2. 0. 0—Timp.—Harp—Strings.
(4). 3. 2. CA. 2. BsCl. 2—4. 0. 0. 0—(?Timp.)—Harp—Strings.
(5). 3. 2. CA. 2. BsCl. 2—4. 2. 3 (Tenors). 1—Timp.—Harp—Strings
(divided).

MS: Autograph full scores (separate songs, with no indication of order)
DT 4 ff 17–71 (RL 30–1), pp. 20, 12, 12, 10, 50. Last 3 items dated 1891.
The order given above is due to TB.

Publication: none. Facsimile of first page of (5), RL 30.

Performance: none recorded.

Words: Alfred, Lord Tennyson (1809–1892):
Maud (1855), part 1, sections xii, ix, xvii, xxi, xxii.

Notes: TB 59–60; Holland 16–17, 52–3.
The last page of a pencil draft for a song ending with the words 'I shall
have had my day' is now bound into DT 39 at f 67 (RL 143). This is the
ending of 'O let the solid ground', also from Tennyson's *Maud*, part I,
xi *see plate 10*.

The 'Tennyson Album', published in 1880, contains a setting (1879) of 3
by Liszt, and one of 5 (1880) by Massenet. Somervell's 'Cycle of [12]
Songs from Tennyson's *Maud*', which includes settings of nos. 1 (5), 3 (6)
and 5 (8), (and also of 'O let the solid ground' (4)) dates from 1898.

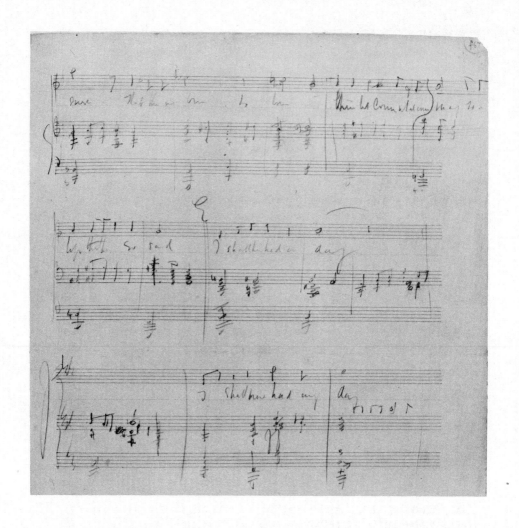

Plate 10: draft of a song ending 'I shall have had my day'

III/4 SEVEN DANISH SONGS
[with orchestral (or pianoforte) accompaniment]

[1.]	Silken Shoes—Seidenschuhe	(F major, C–F)
[2.]	Irmelin [Rose]	(F♯ minor, B–F♯)
[3.]	Summer Nights (On the Sea Shore)	(A♭ major, C–G♭)
[4.]	[In] The Seraglio Garden—Im Garten des Serails	(E♭ major, D♭–G♭)
[5.]	Wine Roses	(C♯ minor, C♯–E)
[6.]	Red Roses (Through long, long years; also, That for which we longed)	(D♭ major, B♭–F)
[7.]	Let Springtime come, then— Den Lenz lass kommen	(A major, C–G♯)

Date: 1897 on MS (*β*), under signature *Frederick Delius*, which indicates a later authentication. The Beecham Libr. list showed a MS (?autograph or copy) of item (4), with pianoforte accompaniment, dated 1894. A letter to Mrs. Jutta Bell, undated but December 1896, speaks of having set five Jacobsen poems.

Dedication: none.

Orchestra: (1). 2. 2. 2. 2—4. 1. 0. 0—Timp. Cym.—Harp—Strings.
(2). 2. 2. 2. 2—4. 2. 0. 0—Timp. (muffled)—Strings (with solo violin).
(3). 0. 0. 0. 0—4 Horns—Strings (divided).
(4). 2. 2. 2. 2—4. 0. 0. 0—(?Timp.) Glockenspiel—Harp—Strings.
(5). 2. 2. 2. 2—4. 0. 0. 0—Trgl. Cym. (both added in first score)—Harp (not in first score)—Strings.
(6). 2. 2. 2. 2—4. 0. 0. 0—Strings.
(7). 2. 2. 2. 2—4. 0. 0. 0—Timp. (added in first score)—Strings.

MS: (*a*). *Orchestral versions*
(*α*). Autograph full score, nos. 6, 7, 2, 3, 5 only, DT 12 ff 1–13 (RL 57) pp. 22, undated, Eng. words only.
(*β*). Autograph full score, complete, DT 12 ff 14–29 (RL 57, 59), pp. 26, dated 1897, Eng. words only.
Both these scores show much evidence of re-numbering the sequence of the songs. The content (and order) of MS (*α*) agrees with that of the first performance in 1899, v. inf., and cf. programme of that concert.
In both MSS, the last eight bars of no. 7 have now been pasted over with an altered version in the hand of Eric Fenby, bearing his authentication of this passage as dictated to him in Grez in 1929. (In answer to my question, he explained that the original had been changed in the piano version prior to publication, but the orchestral score was not then altered to agree; this was done in 1929 in case of subsequent performance, e.g. at the Delius Festival that year. Facsimile of this altered page, GC 36).
The last 2½ bars before 'Poco più vivo' in item 2 (Irmelin Rose) of MS (*β*) appear to have been added later: they do not occur at all in MS (*α*).
The last 6 bars of item 5 (Wine Roses) in MS (*β*) also appear to have been added later, and do not occur in MS (*α*).
MSS of items 2 and 4, also of item 7 (the latter orchestrated by Norman Del Mar) appeared on the Beecham Libr. list.

(*b*). *Pianoforte versions*

1. *Stichvorlage* originally Harmonie-Verlag, according to contract. A MS in Ger. and 'Norwegian' [sic— ?Danish], with the Ger. words in FD's hand, appears on the 1952 list.

2. *Stichvorlage* originally Harmonie-Verlag, according to contract. Another MS, Eng. words only, in a copyist's hand, DT 48a (RL 130), undated, pp. 3, agreeing musically with MS (α) above.

3. Various autograph MSS of preliminary version, DT 36 ff 46, 47b–49 (RL 125, 127); in the original Danish (Lyse Naetter—Paa Stranden) and French ('Mélodies sur des vers de Holger Drachmann (traduit du Danois)') (La plage est silencieuse et déserte); also of the final version in Ger., the latter (Helle Nachte) in Jelka Delius's hand. A copy in Eric Fenby's hand, Eng. words, coll. R. Threlfall.

4. *Stichvorlage* originally Harmonie-Verlag, according to contract. A MS in French & Eng. (and ?Danish too) on 1952 list. ?Another, dated 1894, on Beecham Libr. list.

5. Autograph MS, Danish words, and copyist's copy with Eng. ditto, DT 36 (RL 129, 127). Another copy in Jelka Delius's hand, BL Add. 50497, pp. 3. A copy in Eric Fenby's hand, Eng. words, coll. R. Threlfall.

6. Autograph MS, Danish and Eng. words, and copies by Jelka Delius with Danish/Ger. (by Robert F. Arnold [Jacobsen's Ger. translator]) and Eng./Ger., DT 36 (RL 129–30). A copy in Eric Fenby's hand, Eng. words, coll. R. Threlfall.

7. Copy in Jelka Delius's hand, Ger. only, Oxford University Press, pp. 3. A MS in Danish, Beecham Libr. list. Eng. trans. written by Jelka Delius (without naming translator) into Tischer's proof sheets (Travis and Emery, 1974).

Note: the copies of nos. 3, 5 & 6 by Eric Fenby were made early in 1929, using Delius's own pen for the first time, during the preliminary work for the Delius Festival later that year, and were sent to Philip Heseltine, who particularly admired 'Wine Roses'. (Info. from Eric Fenby). For earlier version(s) of no. 3, see *Lyse Naetter/Dreamy Nights* (song with piano, 1891, p. 107 inf.)

Publication: *Nos. 1, 2, 4* (Silken Shoes; Irmelin; In the Seraglio Garden) (piano versions)

1906, Harmonie-Verlag, Berlin, in *Fünf Lieder* (nos. 3, 5, 2) pp. 8–9, 14–16, 5–7; Ch. 76, Ger. and Eng. text. (Copy in BL, H. 600. f. (4)). See note below re translations.

1921, Universal Edition, Vienna, 3892, ditto. A reprint of above.

1939, transferred to Boosey & Hawkes. Later reprinted unaltered by Boosey & Hawkes Inc. in U.S.A.

1949, Boosey & Hawkes 16557, another reprint.

1977, Boosey & Hawkes, in 20327, Album of D's songs (with some corrections).

Note: see also *Two songs from the Danish,* 1900, p. 113 inf., for further details of these editions.

Orchestral material: Boosey Hire Library.

Nos. 3, 5, 6 (Summer Nights; Wine Roses; Through long, long years) (piano versions).

1973, Galliard (Stainer & Bell) in *Ten Songs* (Five Songs from the Danish, nos. 3, 5, 4) pp. 26–7, 30–2, 28–9, Eng. text only.
Orchestral material: Stainer & Bell Hire Library.

No. 7 (Let Springtime come then) (piano version).

1915, Tischer & Jagenberg, Köln, 251, no. 1 (Frühlingslied: Den Lenz lass kommen) of *Fünf Gesänge* (separately published), Ger. and Eng. text.

1930, Oxford University Press, ditto, a reprint of the above.

1969, Oxford University Press, re-engraved, in *Delius; a Book of Songs*, Set 2, Eng. text only.
Orchestral material: OUP Hire Library.

Facsimile of first page of no. 6, piano version, MM facing p. 85.
Facsimiles of first pages of two MSS of no. 3, piano versions, RL 126.
Facsimile of first page of no. 5, orchestral version, MS (β), RL 58.
Facsimile of portion of no. 6, orchestral version, DLP 34.

Arrangement: (No. 2 only) arranged by Ernest Lubin 'for Eight-Part Chorus of Mixed Voices *a cappella*':

1942, Boston Music Co. 10001, The Choral Art Series 2330, pp. 8. Piano accompaniment 'for rehearsal only'. Eng. text only, 'From the Danish of Jens Jacobsen'.

Performance: of orchestral versions:
nos. 6, 7, 2, 3, 5: 30 May 1899, London, St. James's Hall, Christianne Andray, cond. Alfred Hertz
nos. 1, 4: 16 March 1901, Paris, Société Nationale de Musique, Christianne Andray, cond. Vincent d'Indy.

Words: 1. J. P. Jacobsen, *Digte*, 'Silkesko over gylden Laest' (1873?)
2. J. P. Jacobsen, *Digte*, 'Irmelin Rose' (1869, 1875?)
3. Holger Drachmann, *Songes*, 'Lyse Naetter' (see also p. 107 inf.)
4. J. P. Jacobsen, *Digte*, 'I Seraillets Have' (April 1870)
5. J. P. Jacobsen, *Digte*, 'Løft de klingre Glaspokaler (1874?)
6. J. P. Jacobsen, *Digte*, 'Det bødes der for (1/3/75) [only using the first of the four verses]
7. J. P. Jacobsen, *Digte*, 'Lad Vaaren komme' (1882?)

FD to Ernest Newman, 19 August 1929: *All my Danish songs . . . were first composed in their original language.* The survival of autograph MSS of so many of them with Danish words, albeit in the pianoforte versions —which may well have been the original form—supports this.
The English translations are by Delius himself (see programme of 1899 concert). The Ger. translations are chiefly by Jelka Delius, though one MS. of *Wine Roses* names Robert F. Arnold (Jacobsen's German translator). The French translations sung in Paris in 1901 were made by William Molard. (See also notes to *Two songs from the Danish*, 1900. p. 113 inf.). Frequent alterations appear in the note values, to accommodate differences in the languages concerned.
An attractive translation of no. 2—not, unfortunately, fitting the music— made by Richard Capell appeared in the *Daily Telegraph and Morning Post*, 28 March 1953.

Notes: TB 94–5; Holland 31–4, 53. In a letter to Mrs. Jutta Bell (undated, but December 1896) FD writes: *I have written 5 songs to J. P. Jacobsen's poems.*

In the song *Irmelin*, during the refrain, the accompaniment introduces the key melody from the slightly earlier opera of that name.

An unpublished setting (for voice and piano) of Jacobsen's *In langen Jahren büssen wir* by Arnold Schönberg dates from his earlier (pre-1910) period (Rufer B(6)3). Other settings by him of Jacobsen's words are *Hochzeitslied,* op. 3 no. 4, probably dating from the turn of the century; and of course the huge *Gurrelieder,* commenced in 1900, though not completed and scored until 1911.

III/5 **CYNARA**
for Baritone voice with orchestra. Poem by Ernest Dowson; German text
by Jelka Delius (A–F♯).

Date: drafted 1907, and originally intended for inclusion in 'Songs of
Sunset'; completed in 1929, with the aid of Eric Fenby.

Dedication: 'Dedicated to the memory of Philip Heseltine'.

Orchestra: 3. 2. CA. 3. Bs Cl. 3. Contra—4. 3. 3 (Tenors). 1—Timp.
Xyl. Trgl. Cym.—Harp—Strings.

MS: (*a*). Autograph full score, pencil draft, unfinished, shown on 1935/1
list as 'Sketches (unfinished) for Cynara', and similarly on 1952 list.
Beecham Libr. list gives 'folder containing "Cynara" and MS sketches'.

(*b*). Full score in the hand of Eric Fenby, DT 33 (RL 104), pp. 19, Eng.
only. With Sir Thomas Beecham's performance markings.

(*c*). Fair copy in the hand of Eric Fenby, Boosey & Hawkes archives, pp.
28, Eng. and Ger.
Note: The last 8 bars were added after the first performance, in place of
a simple E major chord. The original pencil draft 'was quite complete in
every detail up to the words "Then falls thy shadow, Cynara", at which
there was a blank', according to a sleeve-note by Eric Fenby.

(*d*). Piano score by Philip Heseltine (1929), autograph MS Boosey &
Hawkes archives, pp. 16; with the last 8 bars (substituting the deleted E
major chord) added by Eric Fenby. Eng. text; Ger. interlined in red by
Jelka Delius.

(*e*). Another (different) piano score, by Eric Fenby, sold by Maggs in
1974 to a USA purchaser. Unpublished.

Publication: 1931, Boosey & Hawkes, piano score by Philip Heseltine, 6961
pp. 11, Eng. and Ger.

1931, Boosey & Hawkes, full score 6964, pp. 23, Eng. and Ger. (this
incorporates Sir Thomas Beecham's markings, see above).

Performance: 18 October 1929. London, Queen's Hall; John Goss, BBC
Symphony Orchestra, cond. Sir Thomas Beecham.

Words: Ernest Dowson, *Verses:*
[Cynara] *Non sum qualis eram bonae sub regno Cynarae* [Horace, Odes
IV, i, 3–4] 4 verses complete; Ger. trans. by Jelka Delius.

Notes: PW 123 n. (112 n.); EF 68–70; TB 207; Holland 20–1, 53.

III/6 **A LATE LARK**
(Die Lerche am Abend)
for Tenor voice with Orchestra
Poem by W. E. Henley; German Text by Jelka Delius.   (C–G)

Date: 1925 (published score); altered to 1924 on MS; completed in 1929 with the aid of Eric Fenby.

Dedication: none.

Orchestra: 1.1. CA. 2.2—2.1. 3 (Tenors). 0—Strings.

MS: (*a*). Draft score, presumed lost. (Complete in draft, EF 70–2; in Jelka Delius's hand, see her letter to Percy Grainger of 23 January '1923' [sic; ?1924]).

(*b*). Full score in the hand of Eric Fenby, DT 33 (RL 105), pp. 5, Eng. text. With Sir Thomas Beecham's performance markings.

(*c*). Fair copy in the hand of Eric Fenby, Boosey & Hawkes archives, pp. 8, Eng. and Ger.

(*d*). Piano score by Eric Fenby, Boosey & Hawkes archives, pp. 10, Eng; Ger. interlined in red by Jelka Delius.

(*e*). A different piano score by Philip Heseltine, MS National Library of Scotland, unpubl.
Note: Eric Fenby explained to me that Heseltine's arrangement was the one originally sent to Heddle Nash for study and rehearsal for the first performance. Fenby and Heseltine 'shared' the making of piano scores of this work and *Cynara;* and it was felt that *Cynara*, more appropriate to Heseltine, be published in his arrangement. On the other hand, Fenby's score of *A Late Lark* was the one issued.

Publication: 1931, Boosey & Hawkes, piano score by Eric Fenby, 6960, pp. 7, Eng. and Ger.

1931, Boosey & Hawkes, full score, 6963, pp. 11, Eng. and Ger. (this incorporates Sir Thomas Beecham's markings, see above).

Performance: 12 October 1929, London, Queen's Hall, Heddle Nash, cond. Sir Thomas Beecham.

Words: William Ernest Henley (1849–1903): *Life and Death (Echoes)*, XXXIV, 1876—Margaritae Sorori (1886).
Ger. trans. by Jelka Delius.

Notes: EF 70–2; TB 207; Holland 21.

Other songs with orchestrated accompaniments are entered and described, under the titles concerned, in section V, Songs with pianoforte accompaniment.

IV Works for unaccompanied voices:

IV/1 [**SIX PART-SONGS** with German texts]
For mixed voices S.A.T.B. unaccompanied.

[1.]	'Lorelei von H. Heine'	(A minor)
[2.]	'Oh! Sonnenschein'	(G major)
[3.]	'Durch den Wald/von Schreck'	(D flat major)
[4.]	'Ave Maria/March 1887'	(E flat major)
[5.]	'Sonnenscheinlied/Björnsen'	(F major)
[6.]	'Frühlingsanbruch/Björnsen'	(C major)

Dates: Item 1, on hand-ruled paper, is evidently the earliest (?1885). This first item has a different style of clefs, and time-signatures (e.g. 2/4) from any other FD MS. Also the words are written, extremely neatly, in German 'schrift', not used by Delius in any other songs. Items 2–3, on American (Carl Fischer) MS paper, probably 1886–7—the styles of clefs and notes and penmanship in general, especially the tails of the quavers, closely resemble those of the dated (1886) MS of *Der Fichtenbaum* (v. inf. p. 89). Item 4 is dated *March 1887* and also exhibits similar characteristics. Items 5–6 possibly 1887 or a little later; here the quaver tails are acute instead of being curved or curly. Beecham dates all 'early 1887' (TB 36).

Dedication: none.

MS: Autographs [is no. 1 autograph?] DT 36 ff 1–9 (RL 115), separate items; only item 4 dated. All with Ger. words only. Alterations and corrections in all except no. 1. This first item is now defective: 1 leaf (=ca. 21 bars), i.e. the finish of the third verse-pair, is missing.
Drafts of items 2, 4 and 5 are to be found in Notebook I, now in Jacksonville University, where an earlier (different) setting of no. 5 also occurs (v. Appendix).
Two draft settings of item 6, the first different but the second agreeing with the final MS, are also to be found in Notebook II, in the Grainger Museum, Melbourne, Australia (v. Appendix).

Publication: items 1, 2, 4: none.
items 6, 5, 3: 1977, Thames Publishing, 'Three Early Part-Songs for unaccompanied chorus (The Coming of Spring; Song of Sunshine; Through the Woods)', pp. 28; edited by Ian Humphris, Eng. singing version by Lionel Carley, piano accompaniment (for rehearsal only) and introduction by R. Threlfall.

Performance: items 3 & 5 only: 11 January 1974, London, St. John's Smith Square; The Linden Singers, cond. Ian Humphris.

Words: (1). Heinrich Heine (1799–1856): *Buch der Lieder,* Die Heimkehr (1823–4), ii, 'Ich weiss nicht was soll es bedeuten'. (Liszt's two settings of this poem for voice and piano date from 1841 and 1856).

(2). Beecham attributes nos. 2–3 to Bjørnson, as well as nos. 5–6 (only in the latter pair do FD's MSS name Bjørnson as poet); but this is unlikely. The first four of the eight lines read as follows: 'Oh Sonnenschein, oh Sonnenschein/Wie schaust du mir ins Herz hinein/Weckt drinnen lauter Liebes Lust/Dass mir so ew'ge wird die Brust.'

(3). 'von Schreck' according to FD's MS. (I have so far been unable to identify these words).

(4). Words untraced so far; (they are NOT, however, those of the pseudo-religious Schubert-Walter Scott song). The first four of the eight lines read as follows: 'Ave Maria, Meer und Himmel ruhn/Vor allen Thürmen hallt der Glocken Ton/Ave Maria, lasst von ird'schen Thun/ Zur Jungfrau betet, zu der Jungfrau Sohn.'

(5). Bjørnstjerne Bjørnson (1832–1910): [Solskinsdagen], from *Arne,* Ch. VIII (1858). Ger. trans. by Edmund Lobedanz. Only the first of the 5 verses is set. (Halfdan Kjerulf set this poem—Solskins-Vise (Sunlight Song)—published with the same Ger. trans. but continuing with the third verse also; it is his op. 6 no. 5).

(6). Words from Edmund Lobedanz's 'Ausgewählte Gedichte von Bj. Björnson und anderen neueren nordischen Dichtern', Leipzig, 1881; Bilder des Jahres, V. Frühlingsanbruch.

Notes: TB 36.

Sketches for another 4-part song, in G minor 6/8, appear in Notebook I; no final copy is known. There also exists in DT 36 ff 10–11 (RL 115) a two-stave draft of another 4-part choral song: 'Herude, herude skal gildet stå' (Ibsen, *Gildet paa Solhaug,* Act II), Norwegian text only, n.d. but probably a little later than some of the above six songs. (See also p. 19–20 above, and Appendix, p. 196).

IV/2, 3, 4 [**THREE UNACCOMPANIED PART-SONGS**]

[1.] On Craig Ddu (An Impression of Nature) [Mountain Silence]/
Bergesstille (Naturszene) for mixed chorus, S.A.T.T.B.B.
[2.] Wanderer's Song/Wanderers Lied for mens chorus, T.T.B.B.
[3.] Midsummer Song/Mittsommerlied for mixed voices, S.S.A.A.T.T.B.B.

Dates: 1. Dec. 1907 on printed score; and see FD to Bantock, 15 December
1907.
2. 1908 on score; FD to Bantock, 28 January 1908: *I have finished another
part song for mens voices.*
3. 1908. FD to Harmonie, 10 April 1908: . . . *since then I have written
a third* [song for choir] . . .

Dedication: none.

MS: Autographs ?originally Harmonie-Verlag, now lost. A MS of no. 3
appears on the Beecham Libr. list.

Publication: 1910, Verlag Harmonie, 344, 345, 343; Ger. and Eng. text, pp.
7, 9. 15. 'Deutsch von R. S. Hoffmann'.

1921, Transferred to Universal Edition; scores, 3910, 3911, 3909; parts—
of *Midsummer Song* only—3909 a–d.

1939/52, Transferred to Boosey & Hawkes Ltd., and reprinted as 17565,
15216, 17655.

Performance: 1. 1910, Blackpool, competition festival.

2.

3. 1910, Whitley Bay and District Choral Society, cond. W. G.
Whittaker.

Words: 1. Arthur Symons (1865–1945): *London Nights,* Colour Studies III
'On Craig Dhu' [sic], August 12, 1892.
2. Arthur Symons: *Images of Good and Evil.* 'Wanderer's Song',
March 10, 1898.
3. (no attribution for words: ?FD)
German texts by R. S. Hoffmann.

Notes: PW 146 (128, 159); TB 169.

That the piano part appearing in the scores is 'for rehearsal only' is clear
from Breitkopf (London)'s letter to Harmonie, 3 August 1909: 'it is
absolutely necessary here for the piano part to be added—just for
practising'.
FD to Bantock, 15 December 1907, states: *the other one I attempted does
not yet please me, so I must live with it a bit longer.*

IV/5 **TO BE SUNG OF A SUMMER NIGHT ON THE WATER**
In einer Sommernacht auf dem Wasser zu singen.
Two unaccompanied Part Songs [without words] for mixed voices,
S.A.T.T.B.B. (and Tenor solo in no. 2).

1. Slow, but not dragging
2. Gaily but not quick

Date: '(late Spring) 1917' on printed score.

Dedication: 'For Kennedy Scott and the Oriana Choir'.

MS: Autograph ?formerly Winthrop Rogers Ltd. MSS also listed on
   Beecham Libr. list. Sketches and drafts are to be found in the 'larger
   small' sketchbook now in the Grainger Museum (see Appendix).

Publication: 1920, Winthrop Rogers, London, 2959, pp. 11. Also Universal
   Edition, Vienna, 7020 (? same—[not seen]).
   Note: the piano part in the score is marked 'for practice only'. A footnote
   to each number concerns the vowel sounds to be employed; also giving
   details concerning breathing and phrasing for performance.

Performance: 28 June 1921, London, Aeolian Hall, Oriana Madrigal
   Society, cond. Charles Kennedy Scott.

Arrangements: (*a*). 'Scored for String Orchestra' (? arranger) MS full score,
   pp. 12, in a copyists hand, Boosey & Hawkes archives, n.d.
   Note: this arrangement differs entirely from (b) below in layout; also no. 1
   is extended by repetition.

   (*b*). TWO AQUARELLES (Deux Aquarelles) (Zwei Aquarell-Farben):
   An arrangement of two unaccompanied Part songs: 'To be sung of a
   summer's night on the water' for String Orchestra, by Eric Fenby.

   MS: full score, pp. 7 oblong, and piano conductor, pp. 4, both in the
   hand of Eric Fenby, Boosey & Hawkes archives; undated, but arranged
   1932 (v. Jelka Delius to Beecham, 16 October 1932).

   Publication: 1938, Hawkes Concert Edition, full score 8021, pp. 10, and
   parts.
   Note: the title 'Aquarelles' stems from Delius himself, according to Eric
   Fenby.

   (*c*). *Two Aquarelles*, arranged for organ by Dom Gregory Murray.
   Published 1938, Boosey & Hawkes, 14803, pp. 5.

Notes: PW (159, 166); TB 188.

IV/6 THE SPLENDOUR FALLS ON CASTLE WALLS

for mixed voices, S.A.T.B. unaccompanied, and '(Separate Chorus [T.B.] to be hummed with a closed mouth imitating horns)'.

Date: 1923, see letter from Jelka Delius to Percy Grainger, 29 November 1923.

Dedication: none.

MS: in the hand of Jelka Delius, ?formerly Oxford University Press, but unlocated in 1974. On the 1952 list, item 5 reads 'Copy MS of 2nd. Violin part of "Appalachia" on which Composer has pencilled score and text of "The Splendour falls on Castle Walls"'.

Publication: 1924, Oxford University Press, London, OCS 252, pp. 8.

Performance: 17 June 1924, London, Aeolian Hall, Oriana Madrigal Society, cond. Charles Kennedy Scott.

Words: Tennyson: *The Princess* (1847), Canto 4.

Note: The piano part in the printed score is marked: 'for rehearsal only'.

V Songs with pianoforte accompaniment:

V/1 WHEN OTHER LIPS SHALL SPEAK

Date: ca. 1880. 'Towards the end of his schooldays at Isleworth' (CD 53).

MS: Autograph (1 page) in the possession of Clare Delius in 1935; subsequent history unknown.

Publication: none.

Words: According to G. Jahoda, *The Road to Samarkand*, Scribner's, New York, 1969, p. 30, the words are by Alfred Bunn, librettist of *The Bohemian Girl*. She quotes 8 lines, which in fact form the first verse of Thaddeus's aria from Act III of that work.

Notes: Not listed in PW; PW (146).
CD 53: '. . . in two parts, the first for a man's voice and the second for a woman's'.

V/2 OVER THE MOUNTAINS HIGH

(C major; C–E)

Date: 1885 (MS).

MS: Autograph, DT 36 f 12 (RL 115), dated *Fritz Delius 1885*. Text in English translation only; strophic, no words under voice part, but words of 4 verses follow the musical text. The MS is written with the fine and very flexible pen only found in a few of the earliest compositions; the quaver tails are curled.

Publication: 1974, in facsimile, RL 116–7 (plates 26–7).

Words: Bjørnstjerne Bjørnson (1832–1910): 'Over de høje Fjaelle', from *Arne*, Ch. XIV (1858), verses 1, 5, 6 & 7 of the 8 verses. (Eng. translator unidentified). The original words were also set by Halfdan Kjerulf (1815–68), op. 6 no. 7 (Over de høje Fjelde) and a number of other composers.

Notes: TB 28; not in PW.

V/3 ZWEI BRÄUNE AUGEN

(G major; B–C♯)

Date: 1885 (MS).

MS: Autograph, Moldenhauer Archive, Spokane, Washington, U.S.A. pp. 2, dated *Fritz Delius 1885*. Text in Ger. only. Written with the same style pen as the previous item.

Publication: none.

Words: Hans Christian Andersen (1805–75): *Digte,* Hjertets Melodier/I: To brune Øjne. Ger. trans. by W. Henzen. The poem was set by Grieg in 1864 as his op. 5 no. 1.

Notes: PW 158 (198); Holland 52.

V/4 DER FICHTENBAUM

(F major; E–F)

Date: 1886 (MS).

MS: Autograph, DT 36 f 27 (RL 122), dated *Fritz Delius 1886*. Text in Ger. only. Also written with the same style pen as the previous two items.

Publication: none.

Words: Heinrich Heine (1799–1856), *Buch der Lieder:* Lyrisches Intermezzo, XXXIII, (1822–3), 'Ein Fichtenbaum steht einsam'. Liszt's two (different) settings of this poem date from 1855 and ca. 1860 respectively.

Notes: TB 36; not in PW.

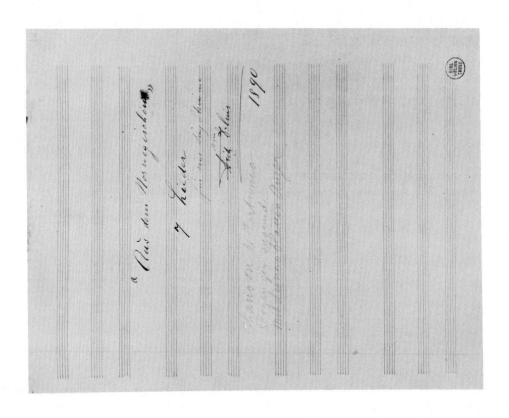

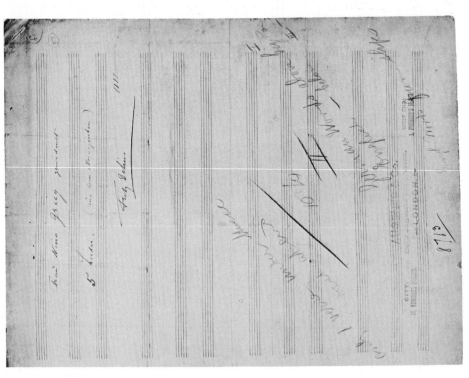

Plate 11: titlepages of 5 Norwegian songs and 7 Norwegian songs.
The publisher's notes on the former; some irrelevant titles by Jelka Delius

90

V/5 **5 LIEDER** (aus dem Norwegischen)
mit Klavierbegleitung von FRITZ DELIUS.

1. Der Schlaf—Slumber Song   (G major; D–F)
2. Sing, Sing—The Nightingale   (E♭ major; B♭–E♭)
3. Am schönsten Sommerabend war's— (F♯ major; D♯/F♯–Fx)
   Summer Eve
4. Sehnsucht—Longing   (D major; A/C♭–F♯)
5. Beim Sonnenuntergang—Sunset (G♭ major; B♭/D♭—G♭)

Date: 1888 according to MS titlepage.

Dedication: 'Frau Nina Grieg gewidmet'.

MS: (*a*) Autograph DT 37 (RL 131–2), pp. 10 (1, 2, 2, 3, 2) plus title page, dated *Fritz Delius 1888*. Original text in German only. Eng. trans. added in red in another hand. Strophic, first verse only under voice part, remainder follow after musical text. The figure '5' on the title-page evidently written over a '6'. *See plate 11.*

(*b*) Copy of no. 1 by Philip Heseltine, Sotheby 16 December 1964 (lot 403); Maggs Cat. 956 March 1974 (lot 139).

Publication: 1890, Augener Limited, London, edition no. 8829 (plate number 8713) pp. 13, Ger. and Eng. words, 'The English words by W. Grist'. Printed with first verse only under voice part and remainder at end. Facsimile of titlepage, DLP 18.

1915, Augener reprinted nos. 1 and 2 with plate nos. 14748–9, with the music set out twice: first verse under the first time, verses 2–3 under the second. No. 2 appeared in the original key, and also transposed up into G major (D–G). Nos. 3, 4 and 5 were offprinted from 8713 in separate issues.

1973, Galliard (Stainer & Bell) in *Ten Songs*, pp. 4–19, containing reprints from 14748–9 (the latter in the transposed key) and 8713, with a few corrections, and introduction by Robert Threlfall.

Words: 1. Bjørnstjerne Bjørnson: *Digte og Sange:* Søvnens Engler (1861). Ger. trans. by Edmund Lobedanz.
2. All editions, also E. Lobedanz's Ger. trans. in his *Ausgewählte Gedichte* (op. cit.), attribute the words of this song to Johan Sebastian Cammermeyer Welhaven (1807–73); according to Halfdan Kjerulf's setting, the words are by Theodor Kjerulf (see letters between the brothers in 1852 also): 'Syng, syng, Nattergal du!' Ger. trans. by Edmund Lobedanz.
3. John Paulsen (1851–1924): 'Jeg reiste en deilig sommerkvaeld'. Ger. trans. by W. Henzen.
4. Theodor Kjerulf (1825–1888): 'Laengsel' (Vildeste Fugl i Flugt). Ger. trans. by Edmund Lobedanz.
5. Andreas Munch (1811–1884): *Nye Digte* (1850): 'Solnedgang' (only verses 1–3 of the 4 stanzas. Ger. trans. by Edmund Lobedanz, as for Grieg's setting (v. inf.)—trans. in Lobedanz's *Ausgewählte Gedichte* differs.
Settings of these poems by other composers are as follows:
1. Halfdan Kjerulf, op. 14 no. 2 [Asleep].
2. Halfdan Kjerulf (no. op. no.).

3. Grieg, op. 26 no. 2 (1876).
4. Halfdan Kjerulf, op. 15 no. 5.
5. Grieg, op. 9 no. 3 (1864); also by N. Gade and others.

Notes: TB 46–7; Holland 14, 23–5.

Note (1)
On the dating of the early Norwegian songs.
It is now probably impossible to give exact individual dates of
composition for the twelve Norwegian Songs first published by Augener,
five in 1890, and seven in 1892. The titlepage of Augener's *Stichvorlage* of
the earlier five bears the date *1888:* it is however to be noted that the '5'
of this title has obviously been altered from a '6'. (An undated [1888]
letter to Grieg from FD, then at St. Malo, states: *I have taken the liberty
of dedicating 6 songs to your dear wife*). This MS is made up as follows:
no. 1 on verso of title; nos. 2 and 3 on separate leaves; followed by a
gathering of 2 double sheets containing nos. 4–5 and 3 blank leaves (v.
RL 132). This make-up could point to a rearrangement before publication.
Delius had sent a number of songs to the Griegs during 1888, *Longing*
being the only one of the titles 'from the Norwegian' mentioned by name
in their surviving correspondence. Later in that year, he asked for the
songs back, *for I should like to make a copy since they are the first ones &
I have not any sketches*. In actual fact, these MSS stayed with the Griegs
until FD visited them later is 1889, when he presumably took his songs
back with him. Other surviving early song fair copies of this and later
periods are individually signed and dated; the lack of such annotation on
the Augener MS, with its collective titlepage, makes this appear to be
the copy he spoke of, and therefore not the original sent in 1888, however
much one would like to think that this early surviving MS (which shows
clear signs of having been folded into four as if to fit the composer's
pocket!) might have been the one sent to the Griegs at the outset of FD's
career. Against this also is an earlier letter from Grieg (23 September
1888) stating: 'by the way she is called Nina, not Lina'; the Augener MS
titlepage (v. plate 11) is headed *Frau Nina Grieg gewidmet* in FD's fairly
unambiguous hand, though it is just possible the N was altered from an L.
In thanking Delius for the songs, in the very same letter, Grieg wrote:
'How strange that I have set to music almost all the same texts'. This
seems to indicate that some of the 'later' Seven Songs (of which Grieg
indeed had set six) were then included, rather than merely the 'earlier'
Five Songs (of which he had only set two). In October that year, FD
spoke of sending other songs to the Griegs, and on 23 November 1888
Grieg acknowledged their safe arrival and expressed his pleasure.
The individual dates of the Seven Songs given in the entry below (p. 95)
are taken from TB 202–4, where no authority for these dates, however,
was given. All the MSS. of these Seven Songs are now missing, as is
perhaps not surprising after their veritable Odyssey among various
publishers. However, the titlepage survives (plate 11), on which one may
note that this time the '7' has probably been altered from a '6',—and
even the date (*1890*) may be a later addition. The only surviving song MS,
on the other half of this double sheet, is *Skogen gir susende* which we
know dates from around that year, though it is not included in either of
the published sets.

In 1890, Delius sent a *volume of songs*—evidently the first Augener printed album—to Grieg and other friends. To Nina Grieg he said: *you know them already,* and Grieg in acknowledgment wrote: 'the one I had not known before is very pretty' (17 June 1890). At the end of 1891, Nina Grieg acknowledged FD's intention to send *the songs* [presumably the second printed volume] *when they are ready*; and her letters of 29 June and 26 October 1892 send her thanks for both songs and further dedication . . . 'I had almost given up "Little Håkon" [*Cradle Song*]; . . . and behold, there he came accompanied by old friends and bringing new ones with him'. It seems likely from this letter, then, that this song, and perhaps some others from the later publication too, were originally included among the earlier groups first sent to Grieg in 1888.

Note (2)
On the language of the original settings of the early Norwegian songs.
Holland (p. 14) states 'All these texts were composed to a German translation', adding (p. 53) that Delius 'in later years regretted that he had not set them in the original language'. In a letter to Ernest Newman on 19 August 1929, however, Delius wrote: *All my Danish Songs and also the Norwegian ones were first composed in their original language,* and the programme book of the second concert of the 1929 Delius Festival states 'All his Scandinavian songs were composed to the original texts'. The surviving evidence, however, appears to support Holland's statement, and to suggest that FD's later memory may have been partly at fault, at least as far as the first two albums of Norwegian songs are concerned.
The full score of the setting of Ibsen's *Paa Vidderne* that Delius was engaged on in 1888 employed the German version of the extensive text; and it was not until mid-1889 that he wrote to Grieg: *I am reading Peer Gynt for the 5th time, this time in Norwegian with help from a dictionary, & am making good progress.* The correspondence between FD and the Griegs is all in German, and there is nothing intrinsically unlikely, in the circumstances, in him setting Norwegian words in a German translation, even if he intended to dedicate the songs to Nina Grieg. No trace of a MS of any of these songs with Norwegian words now survives.
On the flyleaf of a MS setting of Ibsen's *Hochgebirgsleben* (in German only, dated 1888) is a pencil sketch for part of the song *Venevil*. This fragment also has only German words, agreeing with those in the first publication (in the passage in question, later—post-1910—issues altered the German words from those originally set), v. inf. plate 12 and RL 121. Perhaps this fragment may be taken as sufficient evidence, then, that German was the language originally used for these early songs *aus dem Norwegischen,* of which the second set was later reissued as *Seven German Lieder.* In all cases except the setting of Ibsen's *Cradle Song,* FD apparently used the same German texts as were already available to him from translations of settings of the same words by Grieg and Halfdan Kjerulf, all of which would have doubtless been familiar to him at this time. Thus, the apparently opposed statements recorded in the first paragraph above may be reconciled as follows: FD's initial approach to the original words may well have been through these Ger. translations, many of which are also to be found in Edmund Lobedanz's 'Ausgewählte Gedichte . . . nordischen Dichtern' (Leipzig, 1881).

V/6 HOCHGEBIRGSLEBEN

(D♭–F major; D–C′)

Date: 1888 (MS).

MS: Autograph, DT 36 f 13 (RL 115), dated *Fritz Delius 1888*. Text in Ger. only. Two stanzas underlaid to the same notes. Complete, but considerable pencil alterations and overworkings.
Here, an entirely different pen is used, which makes the 'thicks and thins' much more noticeable, e.g. in the slurs and the quaver beams. (This style persists for the next 3 years or so).

Publication: 1974, in facsimile, RL 118–9 (plates 28–9).

Words: Henrik Ibsen (1828–1906); *Digte:* Høifjeldsliv (1859). Delius set L. Passarge's Ger. trans. only of the first two of Ibsen's five stanzas, in strophic form.

Notes: TB 47; not in PW. Beecham refers to the song as 'Now sinks the summer evening'; the opening words of the Ger. version set are 'Nun ruht der Sommerabend lind'.

V/7 'O SCHNELLER MEIN ROSS'
'Plus vite mon cheval'

(D major; D–G/B♭′)

Date: 1888 (MS).

Dedication: 'à Madame la P^esse de Cystria' in some printed copies; this was probably added to the plate later, as the dedication does not appear in the Bibl. Nat. copy.

MS: Copyist's MS, DT 36 ff 20–22 (RL 122), n.d., signed [later] *Frederick Delius,* Ger. only. A MS with French title, probably autograph, dated, Beecham Libr. list.

Publication: 1896, L. Grus fils, Editeur, 116 B^d Hartmann, Paris; no. 4 of '5 Chansons. . . Musique de Fritz Delius. . .' FD4, Fr. and Ger. text. At foot of last page: 'Mme Roussel, Grav. Imp. E. Delay, rue Rodier 49'. Copy in Bibl. Nat. Vm^7 14547. Facsimile of titlepage, DLP 32.

Words: Emmanuel Geibel (1815–1884), *Gedichte:* 'Lieder als Intermezzo', XXXVIII. Only the first 3 of the 6 quatrains are set by Delius.

Notes: TB 47; PW 162 (202) wrongly dated. Both state 'later withdrawn by the Composer'.
FD to Mrs. Jutta Bell, 15 July 1896: *5 of my songs have come out in Paris, of which 2 new ones . . .* ditto, n.d. [Dec 1896]: *I will send you some of my new songs when they arrive from Paris.*
Grieg to FD, 23 November 1888: 'The Geibel poem "O schneller mein Ross" is splendid!'
The words were erroneously attributed to Verlaine by Grove V, doubtless the result of a typographical ambiguity in PW 162.
An earlier setting of these words by the young Richard Strauss, dating from 1879, was performed from the MS but subsequently lost.

V/8 CHANSON [DE] FORTUNIO

(G major; B♭–F♯)

Date: 'Croissy, le 12 Novembre 1889'.

MS: Autograph, DT 36 ff 37–8 (RL 123), dated as above, and signed *Fritz Delius*. Text in French only. The musical handwriting resembles that of *Hochgebirgsleben* in all characteristics.

Publication: 1975, in facsimile, LKC [87–89].

Words: Alfred de Musset (1810–1857): *Le Chandelier,* Act II, Scene 3.

Notes: TB 47; not in PW.

V/9 7 LIEDER (aus dem Norwegischen)
mit Klavierbegleitung von FRITZ DELIUS.

1. Wiegenlied—Cradle Song	(D♭ major; C–F)
2. Auf der Reise zur Heimat [later: Heimkehr]— The Homeward Journey	(A♭ major; E♭–F)
3. Abendstimmung—Evening Voices [later: Twilight Fancies]	(B minor; D–F♯)
4. Kleine Venevil—Sweet Venevil	(C major; C–G)
5. Spielleute [later: Spielmann]—Minstrel	(F♯ minor; C♯–F♯)
6. Verborg'ne Liebe—Love concealed	(F major; D–A)
7. Eine Vogelweise—The Birds Story	(F major; D(A)–G)

Date: 1889–90 (PW); nos. 1, 2, 3, 7 1889; 5, 6 1890; 4 1889–90 (TB 202–4).

Dedication: 'Frau Nina Grieg gewidmet'.

MS: Autographs lost. Uncertain if returned to FD by Augener in 1895 (v. inf.); at time of Tischer reissue (1910) the contract specified 'the MSS, insofar as these are still available, become the property of the publishers'. These MSS were not among those returned by Augener Ltd. to the DT in 1964, nor were they with the present owners, Oxford University Press, in 1974.
Titlepage (?) 1890 and fragment of a draft of no. 4, DT 36 ff 15, 14b (RL 121), *'Aus dem Norwegischen'/7 Lieder/für eine Sing Stimme/von/Fritz Delius/1890*. The figure '7' probably altered from a '6'; the date possibly added later. *See plates 11 and 12.*

Publication: 1892, Augener Limited, London, edition no. 8829b (plate number 9489) pp. 29, Ger. and Eng. words; the English words by Wm. Archer [no. 1] and W. Grist [nos. 2–7]. The music not repeated in nos. 2 and 4; both verses written under the voice line. Copy in BL G.385. i. (5). In 1895 the plates, copyright of the Eng. words and some printed sheets were transferred back to FD; Augeners retaining some stock, as the work remained advertised in their catalogue.

1896, L. Grus fils, Paris, nos. 1 (Berceuse) and 5 (La ballade du musicien) only; the latter transposed down into E minor, in '5 Chansons... de Fritz Delius', FD 1–2, French and Ger. words. Copies in Bibl. Nat. Vm^7 14547.

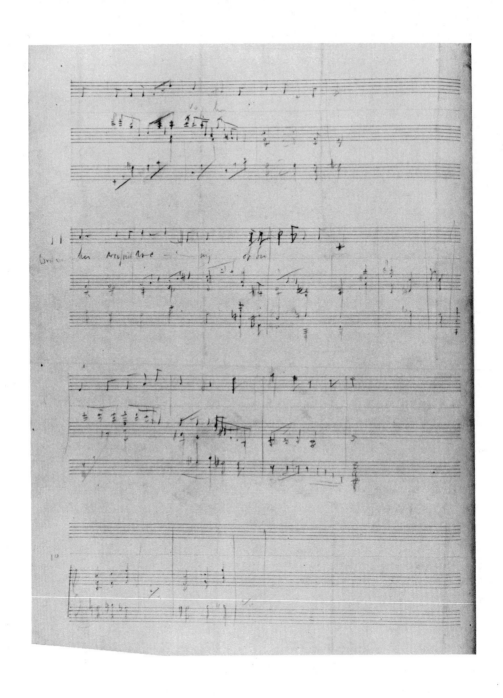

Plate 12: song *Venevil*: an early sketch page

1899, in *The Dome,* Vol. 3 (June) 1899, pp. 99–103, no. 6 only, 'reproduced by arrangement', Ger. and Eng. text (same as Augener issue).

1899, complete, reissued in separate numbers by The Concorde Concert Control, 'Seven German Lieder by Fritz Delius', Ger. and Eng. texts, same plates as Augener issue but no numbers and new cover/title (slate-blue wording) and with facsimile signature stamped on front cover, 'Printed by F. M. Geidel, Leipzig'. Copies in BL I. 525. v. (5). See *Notes* inf. re issues from Stanley Lucas Weber [and Pitt &] Hatzfeld.

post-1903 [see *Notes* inf.], complete, reissued in separate numbers by Breitkopf and Härtel, London, as 'Frederick Delius SONGS. Seven German Lieder', Ger. and Eng. texts, same plates as Augener issue but cover/title black on silurian duplex paper. Copies in BL G. 805.hh. (37).

1910, 'The remainder of the editions which have already appeared . . . have been taken over by the publisher, Tischer & Jagenberg' [acc. to contract]. Subsequently, re-engraved and reissued as follows by Tischer & Jagenberg, Cologne: (nos. 5, 7, 1) '3 Lieder, Dichtungen von Henrik Ibsen', T. & J. nos. 10, 11, 12, pp. 16, Ger. and Eng. texts (Brown and gold on ribbed buff paper wrappers). (nos. 3, 4, 6) '3 Lieder, Dichtungen von Bj. Björnson', T. & J. nos. 13, 14, 15, pp. 13, orig. Ger. text only; later Ger. and Eng. (Blue and gold on ditto). (no. 2) 'Heimkehr, Dichtung von Assmus O. Vinje', T. & J. no. 22, Ger. and Eng. text (Mauve on ditto). No. 2 has a new Ger. trans. by G. Tischer; there are also some alterations to the German in nos. 1, 4, 5 & 7 (? also by Dr. Tischer, v. inf.). The Eng. words of no. 1 by Wm. Archer; of nos. 2, 3 and 7 certainly and nos. 4, 5 and 6 possibly by F. S. Copeland originally, some further alterations being made later (v. inf.). Also all issued in separate copies.
For this re-engraving, the music of the last line of each verse of no. 2 was slightly altered and compressed; the piano part of the second half of each verse of nos. 3 and 4 and the ending of no. 6 were also altered, the latter only very slightly; nos. 2 and 4 were now written out in full.

1930, the Tischer editions were all transferred to Oxford University Press, London; who reprinted in separate copies (with covers in their own house style) as and when stocks ran out; and also issued a transposed version of no. 3 in G minor (B♭–D) [1949].

1969, Re-engraved by Oxford University Press for inclusion in 'Delius, A Book of Songs', Sets 1 (nos. 1 and 3–7) and 2 (no. 2), Eng. words only; all except no. 3 retranslated by Peter Pears. Most of the errors of earlier editions corrected. No. 3 only from this edition reprinted in *Music and Musicians*, July 1971, pp. 42–5.

Words: 1. Henrik Ibsen: Vuggevise (from *Kongs-Emnerne* [The Pretenders] Act III), Ger. by L. Passarge
2. Aasmund O. Vinje (1818–70): *Ferdaminni* (1861), Ved Rundarne   Ger. by Edmund Lobedanz
3. Bj. Bjørnson: *Digte og Sange*, Aftenstemning (Prinsessen) (1861)   Ger. by F. von Holstein

4. Bj. Bjørnson: *Arne*, Ch. IX,
Venevil, vv. 1–2 of the 7 verses,   Ger. by Edmund Lobedanz
5. H. Ibsen: *Digte*,
Spillemaend (1851) (all 4 verses)   Ger. trans. by L. Passarge,
                                                     differs from that by W.
                                                     Henzen for Grieg's setting, v.
                                                     inf.

6. Bj. Bjørnson: *Digte og Sange*,
Dulgt kjaerlighed (Romance) (1862)   Ger. by W. Henzen
7. H. Ibsen: *Digte*, En fuglevise (1858)
(all 7 verses)   Ger. by L. Passarge.

Six of these seven poems were previously set by Grieg as follows: nos. 1,
op. 15 no. 1 (1868); 2, op. 33/II no. 3 (1880); 3 (no op. no.) (1871); 5, op.
25 no. 1 (1876); 6, op. 39 no. 2 (1872–3); 7, op. 25 no. 6 (1876). Nos. 3,
4 and 6 were also set by Halfdan Kjerulf (Evensong, op. 14 no. 1;
Venevil, op. 6 no. 6; A Secret, op. 14 no. 3; Ger. by Edmund Lobedanz
for all 3) as also by many other composers.

Notes: TB 54; Holland 14–15, 25–30, 53–4.
A song dated 1890 and entitled 'Wohl waren es Tage' was shown on the
Beecham Libr. list.
For an earlier sketch of no. 1, see Appendix: Notebook III.
Correspondence between FD and Mrs. Jutta Bell in 1899, after the Delius
concert on 30 May, refers to the stamping of each song copy with his
facsimile signature, both those published by Norman Concorde *& those to
be published by Stanley-Lucas on a royalty*. He later asked Mrs. Bell to
get the stamp and stamp all the songs *& also those coming out from
Hatzfeldt* [sic]. By 30 June, she had stamped 3000 copies (!) of the songs,
and FD wrote *I wonder what Stanley-Lucas are doing with my songs*. (10
separate songs were concerned—7 Norwegian and the 3 Shelley songs—
and 300 copies of each may not have been unreasonable). At this date,
the firm concerned was 'Stanley Lucas, Weber, Pitt & Hatzfeld Ltd.'
Whether they issued any of the songs in question themselves, or whether
they also distributed the Concorde issues, I have not yet been able to
establish.
FD changed his name 'Fritz' to 'Frederick' at the time of his marriage in
1903; the Breitkopf publication, then, must postdate this event. On the
other hand, a letter to Bantock (n.d. but November 1907) states: *I sent
you 3 songs today and will send you some more tomorrow. Kling* [Breitkopf]
will undertake the sale of these songs. Does this mean that the Breitkopf
issue was as late as 1907?
Drafts (in German, by Jelka Delius) of letters to Sander (Leuckart) and
Tischer in June 1910 state that Breitkopf and Härtel were handling the
songs because the previous publisher had gone broke. FD apparently
gave Sander the first refusal before sending the songs to Dr. Tischer for
a new edition, *as they are still quite unknown in Germany*.
The following extracts from letters written to Dr. G. Tischer are also
instructive:
1908. *An edition de luxe does not appeal to me very much*.
13 July 1910: *The English translations of the songs are so bad that I do
not wish to have them published again . . . you must have a new translation
prepared*.

(n.d.) *In one song I have a small alteration to make—Venevil*
24 July 1910: *... very pleased that you will bring out the songs so beautifully ... Blue-gold should look very well on parchment.*
29 July 1910: detailed discussion of Dr. Tischer's revisions, especially of no. 2; no. 4 now altered and the accompaniment simplified: *Please print the two verses separately and please insert the dynamic variations yourself.* A retranslation into Eng. (by W. Wallace) of no. 3 is suggested, and minor comments made to nos. 5 and 7.
31 August 1912: *... there is a whole lot of very comic mistakes in the English words ... For example ... wat instead of what, blozing instead of blazing ... wondered instead of wandered ... trough instead of through (trough means Viehtrog). As it is there, it will only make a laughing stock of me ... For Heaven's sake do not send this edition to England or America. That was obviously corrected by one of the many Germans who are 'proficient in English'.*
As late as 1929, we find a letter to Dr. Tischer on 12 May sending *the improved songs* and evidently referring to changes in the English words (by Jelka Delius) for a new impression [an early translator of this letter attributed these Eng. words to Neustich. . . .]. The seven songs (as later offprinted by Oxford University Press) incorporate these amendments, but still retain F. S. Copeland's name at the head of nos. 2, 3 and 7 as translator.

Orchestral versions: of nos. 3 and 7 by FD, 1908, for Olga Wood
(Liverpool, perf. 21 March; Birmingham 25 March; see HJW 312, giving incorrect date as 1909). MSS, Beecham Libr. list; copies RAM (Sir Henry Wood library). Orch: no. 3—2. 2. CA. 2. 2—4. 0. 0. 0—Strings; no. 7—2. 2 (CA). 2. 2—4. 1. 0. 0—Timp.—Harp—Strings; material, Oxford University Press hire library.

Also, nos. 1 and 4 orchestrated 'by or for Sir Thomas Beecham' (Holland, 54); no. 2 orchestrated by R. Sondheimer (programme, Delius Festival, London, Central Hall, 21 November 1946) and no. 3 orchestrated Thomas Beecham (ibid. 18 November 1946). MSS Beecham Libr. unpubl.

V/10 **'SKOGEN GIR SUSENDE LANGSOM BESKED'**
$$(F\sharp \text{ minor}; C\sharp-F\sharp)$$

Date: 1890 or 1891, see notes below.

MS: Autograph, DT 36 f 18 (RL 121), undated, Norwegian words only. An autograph of the first 4 bars, voice part and words only, signed *Fritz Delius, Aulestad, le 11 Juillet 91,* Oslo University (RL 120–1).
The DT MS is on the other leaf of the titlepage to the *Seven Norwegian Songs,* v. supra, which bears the date 1890. The musical penmanship, perhaps for the last time, exhibits the 'thick and thin' characteristics mentioned above (v. *Hochgebirgsleben,* 1888).

Publication: none as yet.

Words: Bjørnstjerne Bjørnson; quoted in his letter of 30 March 1890 to his daughter Bergliot, then in Paris. The poem was actually written considerably earlier, but was subsequently mislaid, and later included in *Digte og Sange* as 'I Skogen'.

Notes: LKC 27–8. Not in PW.
Whether this setting dates from the time of FD's visit to the poet in July 1891, or whether the verse was given to him to set by Bergliot Bjørnson shortly after she received it from her father (who said in his letter to her 'someone should set it to music'), remains uncertain.

V/11 [SONGS TO WORDS BY HEINE]

[1.] Mit deinen blauen Augen	(F major; D–A)
[2.] Ein schöner Stern geht auf in meiner Nacht	(B major; E♯–G♯)
[3.] Hör' ich das Liedchen klingen	(A♭ major; E♭–A♭)
[4.] Aus deinen Augen fliessen meine Lieder	(D♭ major; E♭–G♭)

Date: 1890–1, according to MSS of item 3; probably all contemporaneous.

MS: Separate autographs of 1–3 and copyist's copy of 4, DT 36 ff 28, 29–31, 32–34, 35–36 (RL 122–3). Item 1 in draft form only; item 2 in draft and fair copy; item 3 in two versions, one dated 1890 and the other 1891. Items 1, 2 & 4 n.d. Ger. words only.
Here, for the first time in the songs, a harder pen is used. Not only are the quaver beams less thick, but in this style the bass clefs are made 'backhand' from now on.

Publication: Nos. 1 and 2: *see plates 13–14*.
Nos. 3 and 4: unpublished.

Words: Heinrich Heine:
1. *Neue Gedichte*, Neue Frühling, XVIII (1828–31).
2. *Neue Gedichte*, Verschiedenes, Katharina, I.
3. *Buch der Lieder*, Lyrisches Intermezzo, XL (1822–3).
4. (I have so far been unable to trace this poem amongst the works of Heine). The first of the four verses reads as follows: 'Aus deinen Augen fliessen meine Lieder/aus keiner andern Quelle schöpf ich mehr/Ich blick hinein und wieder immer wieder/spriesst jubelnd draus hervor ein Liederheer.'

Settings of these poems by other composers are as follows:
1   Richard Strauss, op. 56 no. 4 (1903).
3 { R. Schumann, op. 48 (Dichterliebe) no. 10 (1840).
  { Edvard Grieg, op. 39 no. 6 (1885).

Notes: TB 60; not in PW.
In Notebook II, now in the Grainger Museum, is a drafted setting of Heine's 'Warum sind denn die Rosen so blass' (*Buch der Lieder*, Lyrisches Intermezzo, XXIII). See Appendix and SM7, 74.

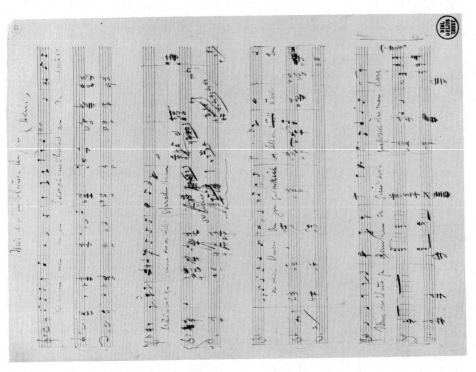

Plate 13: (a) Draft of a song: *Mit deinen blauen Augen* (Heine)
(b) Song: *Ein schöner Stern* (Heine) (beginning)

102

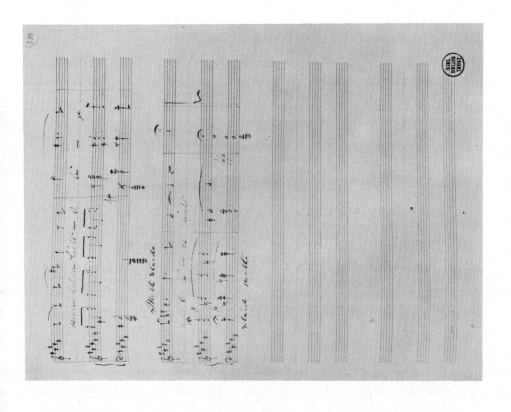

103

Plate 14: Song: *Ein schöner Stern* (continuation and end)

V/12 **3 SONGS**
The words by SHELLEY
The music by FRITZ DELIUS

1. Indian Love Song   (E♭ major; E♭–B♭)
2. Love's Philosophy   (G major; D♯–G)
3. To the Queen of my Heart (B major; D♯–A♯)

Date: 1891 (PW, TB).

MS: Autographs lost. See note to MSS of 7 Lieder of 1889–90, p. 95. A
MS of no. 1 appears on the Beecham Libr. list.

Publication: 1892, Augener Limited, edition no. 8824 (plate no. 9442),
pp. 19, Eng. words only. Transferred back to FD in 1895, as in the case of
the 7 Lieder of 1889–90, q.v. Copy in BL G. 385. i. (3).

1896, L. Grus fils, Paris, no. 1 only, transposed down into C major, in
'5 Chansons . . . de Fritz Delius', no. 3, FD3, French and Eng. words.
Copy in Bibl. Nat. Vm[7] 14547. ("Chant Indien").

1899, Reissued complete, but in separate numbers, by The Concorde
Concert Control, 'Three English Songs (poems by Shelley)', same plates
as Augener but no numbers, as in the case of the 7 Lieder. Copies in
BL I. 525. v. (4).

post-1903, Reissued complete, but in separate numbers, by Breitkopf and
Härtel, London, as 'Frederick Delius . . . Three English Songs', same
plates as Augener, as above. Copies in BL G. 1044. b. (3).

1910, Transferred to Tischer & Jagenberg, Cologne, who at first
continued to use 'Augener' sheets but in their own fawn ribbed wrapper,
printed in red and gold. Subsequently re-engraved and reissued complete
as follows:
'Drei Lieder. Dichtungen von Percy B. Shelley: Indisches Liebeslied/
Liebesphilosophie/An meines Herzens Königin', T & J 16, 17, 18, pp. 19
Ger. and Eng. text (Ger. trans. of 1 and 2 by Jelka Rosen; of 3 by G.
Tischer). Also issued in separate numbers. Later, separate copies had an
English cover, but retained the Ger. titlepage.

1930, Tischer editions transferred to Oxford University Press, London,
who reprinted in separate copies (with covers in their own house style) as
and when stocks ran out.

1969, Oxford University Press, in *A Book of Songs*, Set 2, re-engraved,
with Eng. words only.

Words: Percy Bysshe Shelley (1792–1822):
1. The Indian Serenade (1822) ⎱ from *Posthumous Poems*, 1824.
2. Love's Philosophy (1819)   ⎰
3. To the Queen of my Heart, from *Poetical Works*, 1839. (Authenticity
of no. 3 doubtful?).

Notes: TB 59; Holland 16, 44–6, 54.
FD to Dr. G. Tischer, 24 July 1910: *I had to sell the three Shelley songs to
Novello* [sic] *before as I needed money. I am nevertheless ready, if you
would like . . . to cede them to you . . .* Writing to the same on 22 August,
FD refers to *your splendid translation of 'To the Queen of my Heart'*. On
25 September, however, he rejected the translations of the other two

104

items, with detailed discussion. Writing on 8 October, FD says: *Please accept these two texts by my wife.*

See also FD's letter on this subject to Ernest Newman on 19 August 1929: *Of course I composed* [To the Queen of my Heart] *in english and only reluctantly allowed a translation to be printed at all. . . . battling against the publishers, who wish to print the words in their own language over the others . . . If certain editions have been put on the market like that it is entirely against my will.*

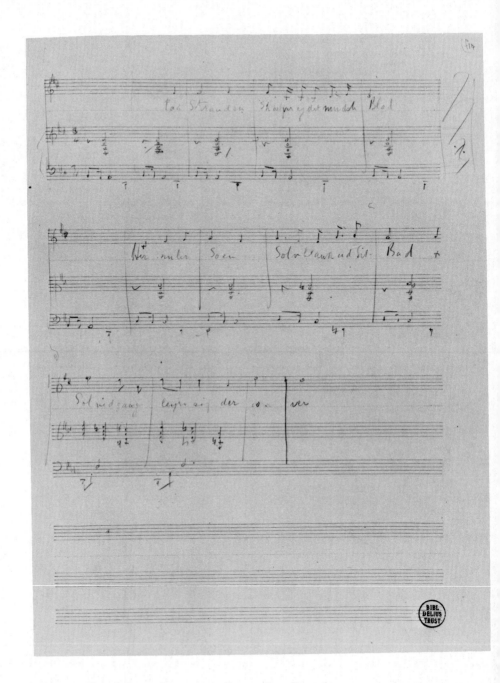

Plate 15: Sketch for early version of song: *Paa Stranden*

V/13 **LYSE NAETTER**
Dreamy Nights (E♭ major: C–G)

Date: 1891 (MS)

MS: (*a*). Sketch of *first* version, incomplete, DT 36 f 14 (RL 121), n.d.
Danish words only, *see plate 15*.

(*b*). *Second* version, autograph DT 36 ff 42–3 (RL 124–5), dated 1891,
Danish words only; the latter part only in draft.

(*c*). ditto, autograph DT 36 ff 44–5 (RL 124–5), undated, Danish words
and Delius's own Eng. trans. This MS is complete.
Note: the commencement of the dated MS(b) has the 'thick and thin'
characteristics already noted; the other MS(c) exhibiting the harder pen
and backhand bass clefs seen in other songs of this period and later.

(*d*). MS copy, probably in the hand of Jutta Bell, Jacksonville University;
dated 'Paris 1903' and with a 'better translation' at end, over her
signature.

Publication: 1973, Galliard (Stainer & Bell), in *Ten Songs* (Five Songs from
the Danish, no. 2), Eng. text (by FD) only.

Words: Holger Drachmann; *Ungdom i Digt og Sang* (1879), Døgnets
Psalmer (Nye Sange ved Havet).

Notes: TB 60; not in PW. Beecham refers to this song by the opening
words: 'On shore how still, all Nature seems asleep' [Paa Stranden].
The later, and ultimately *final*, version of FD's setting of these words,
completed by 1897, appears as 'Summer Nights' (On the Sea Shore), no.
3 of *Seven Danish Songs* with orchestral or pianoforte accompaniment,
v. supra p. 77–8.

V/14 'JEG HAVDE EN NYSKAAREN SELJEFLØJTE'

(G♮ major; A–G♮)

Date: 1892 or 93, see notes below.

MS: Autograph, DT 36 ff 16–17 (RL 121), undated. Norwegian text only.
The handwriting is with the 'harder' pen first noticed about the 1890s.

Publication: none as yet.

Words: Vilhelm Krag (1871–1933): *Digte* (1891) (?) (these lines do not
appear in the standard editions, however).

Notes: LKC 49; not in PW.
A copy of Krag's *Digte* was given to Delius by the Griegs at Christmas
1891. He met the poet in Paris in 1893, and it seems likely that his only
setting of verse by this writer should date from that period.

V/15 NUAGES

(D♭ major; E–G♭).

Date: 1893 (MS).

MS: (*a*). Autograph, DT 36 ff 39–40 (RL 123), dated *Fritz Delius 1893*.
French text only.

(*b*). MS copy, probably in the hand of Jutta Bell, Jacksonville University;
with 'not published' and her signature at end.

Publication: 1975, in facsimile, LKC [90–92].
The first page of the Jacksonville MS copy was reproduced in facsimile
on the cover of a Delius Memorial Concert programme, Jacksonville,
Fla., USA, 2 February 1951.

Words: Jean Richepin (1849–1926):

Notes: LKC 33; not in PW.

V/16 **DEUX MÉLODIES**
Poésies de Paul Verlaine

1. Il pleure dans mon coeur   (C♯–F♯)
2. Le ciel est, par-dessus le toit (D♭–F♭)

Date: 1895 (PW)

MS: (*a*). Autograph, no. 2 only, DT 48a (RL 130), 'Melodie sur des vers de Paul Verlaine', n.d. unsigned. Now a revised state; the original conclusion having been partly pasted over (using similar paper) but partly surviving on f 47a of DT 36 (RL 127). Facsimile of a few bars in DLP 30.

(*b*). *Stichvorlagen*, in the hand of a copyist, DT 48a, n.d. Ger. trans. by, and interlined in the hand of, G. Tischer. Some alterations to the Ger. may be in the hand of Jelka Delius; there are also several differences in the printed publication.

Publication: 1896, (No. 1 only). L. Grus fils, Paris; no. 5 of '5 Chansons . . . de Fritz Delius', FD5, French text only.

1896, (No. 2 only). *L'Aube*, Paris, no. 4, 1ᵉ année, juillet 1896, 'Mélodie de F. Délius/sur des vers de Paul Verlaine', French text only. (v. note below).

1910, (Nos. 1 & 2). Tischer & Jagenberg, Cologne, 19–20; nos. 1 (Regenlied) and 2 (Der Himmel ruht dort überm Dach) of 'Drei Lieder, Dichtungen von P. Verlaine', pp. 2–7, French and Ger. words (Ger. trans. by G. Tischer) (for no. 3, see *La Lune blanche*, p. 116 inf.). Later issued separately. Wrapper fawn, printed green and gold.
Note: no. 1 differs very slightly from the first edition of L. Grus; no. 2 differs considerably in the last 11 bars from the first edition listed above, v. inf.

1930, Transferred to Oxford University Press, London.

1969, ditto, in *A Book of Songs*, set 2, re-engraved, French words only.

Words: Paul Verlaine (1844–96):
1. *Romances sans paroles*, Ariettes oubliées, III (1874).
2. *Sagesse*, III/6 (1881).
Other settings of these words:
1. by Claude Debussy, Ariettes [oubliées] no. 2, 1888.
2. by Reynaldo Hahn, 'D'une prison', 1895.
   by Gabriel Fauré, 'Prison', op. 83 no. 1, 1900.
   by Igor Stravinsky, op. 9 no. 2, 1910.

Notes: Holland 37–9.
The early (first) publication of no. 2 in *l'Aube* agrees with the presumed original state of the MS now in DT 48a (i.e. before it was pasted over with the later version), concluding with the bars now in DT 36, f 47a. I am indebted to M. Jean-Michel Nectoux, Département de la Musique, Bibliothèque Nationale, for tracing this very rare issue and supplying a photograph thereof. It is to the later published version of these last bars, not to the first edition, that Beecham's eloquent mention (TB 83) refers.

The *Stichvorlage* above, originally agreeing with the autographs (of no. 2 above, as amended and the missing no. 1) has been altered slightly as necessary to establish the text engraved by Tischer & Jagenberg.

FD to Dr. Tischer, 13 July 1910: *The French songs must in no case be translated into English.* Some alterations to Tischer's Ger. trans. were proposed in a letter from FD to him on 30 July 1910.

Orchestral version: by FD; a MS, Beecham Libr. list, unpubl. PW 202–3 (2.2.2.2—4.0.0.0—Timp.—Solo violin & Strings).

No. 1 performed 25 January 1915, London, Grafton Galleries, Jean Waterston.

Note: In an undated letter, probably of this period, Georgette Leblanc asked Delius to set to music a poem by her husband, Maurice Maeterlinck; and Delius apparently agreed. See LKC 62.

V/17 'PAGEN HØJT PAA TAARNET SAD'
The Page sat in the lofty Tower

(G minor; D–A♭)

Date: (?1895)

MS: Autographs, DT 36 ff 76–7 and 78–9 (RL 129), n.d. Danish and Eng. words. A copy in the hand of Jelka Delius has Ger. words also (ff 80–1).

Publication: 1973, Galliard (Stainer & Bell), in *Ten Songs* (Five songs from the Danish, no. 1), English text (by FD) only.

Words: Jens Peter Jacobsen, *Digte:* 'Genrebillede' (1875?).

Notes: not in PW.
As regards the date, it is to be noted that on the verso of the fair copy, f 79 above, in DT 36, is the commencement of what was originally a fair copy of the preliminary setting of the final version of *Lyse Naetter* (v.p. 77); the remainder of this MS is now DT 36 f 16, on the same leaf as the commencement of *Jeg havde en nyskaaren Seljefløjte*.
The letter of [Dec 1896] to Mrs. Jutta Bell quoted above (v. *Seven Danish Songs*, p. 80) speaks of 5 Jacobsen songs being written; it seems likely that the song here considered was one of these, but that it failed to gain admission to the definitive set.

Note: the *Seven Danish Songs* of 1897 exist in versions with pianoforte and with orchestral accompaniment. Both versions are considered together, under the general heading 'Solo voice and orchestra', pp. 77–80 above.

V/18 TRAUM ROSEN

(E♮ major: B♭–E♭)

Date: ca. 1898.

MS: Autograph, DT 36 ff 23–4 (RL 122), n.d. and unsigned. Also a copyist's copy ff 25–6, signed (evidently later) *Frederick Delius* and with the poet's name given as '(Marie Heinitz)'.

Publication: 1976, in *The Delius Society Journal,* London, April 1976, No. 51 (facsimile of a transcript in the hand of R. Threlfall).

Words: Marie Heinitz (formerly Marie Krönig, widow of Delius's cousin Arthur Krönig).

Notes: TB 47; not in PW. (TB implies the date to be 1888).
See also Delius Society Journal, loc. cit, 'Dating a Delius Song' by Lionel Carley and Robert Threlfall.

V/19 [VIER] LIEDER NACH GEDICHTEN VON FRIEDRICH NIETZSCHE
für mittlere Stimme und Klavier

1. Nach neuen Meeren   (C♯ minor; D–F♯)
2. Der Wanderer   (G minor; B–G)
3. Der Einsame   (D♭ major; D–G)
4. Der Wanderer und sein Schatten (C♯ minor; C–E)

Date: 1898 (PW).

MS: Autograph untraced (? originally with Publishers). MSS of nos. 2 and 4 on Beecham Libr. list.

Publication: . . . ? Leuckart, Leipzig (Draft letter 25 June 1913, FD to Leuckart refers to *ein noch z. liefernd Heft 5 Lieder*).

1924, Universal Edition 6896, pp. 7. Ger. words only.

1977, Boosey & Hawkes, in 20327 Song Album.

Words: Friedrich Nietzsche:
1. from *Die Fröhliche Wissenschaft* (1882), Anhang, Lieder des Prinzen Vogelfrei.
2. ditto, Vorspiel in deutschen Reimen (Scherz, List und Rache), 27.
3. ditto, 33.
4. *Menschliches, Allzumenschliches* (1878), Ein Buch für freie Geister; zweiter Band, zweiter Abteilung.

Notes: PW 204; Holland 19–20, 42–3, 52.
See also notes to next item: *Im Glück wir lachend gingen.*

V/20 IM GLÜCK WIR LACHEND GINGEN

Date: 1898 (PW).

MS: Autograph untraced.

Publication: ?Leuckart (v. inf.).

Words: Holger Drachmann: probably 'Vi lo jo før saa laenge/Og spandt paa Glaedens Traad', *Ungdom i Digt og Sang* (1879), Sange til en Søster, 9. Ger. trans. ? by Jelka Delius.

Notes: PW 166 (204).
Holland 52 states 'The volume of Nietzsche-Lieder, published by Leuckart, originally contained a fifth song, *Im Glück wir lachend gingen* (Drachmann), which was withdrawn from publication when the copyright was acquired after the first war by Universal-Edition'.
Enquiries with Leuckart in 1972 failed to trace any copy, printed or MS; or any concrete evidence of publication by that firm. Maybe it did not go beyond the proof-sheet stage?
I have, therefore, been unable to trace any copy of this most elusive of FD's published songs, in any form, so far.

V/21 [TWO SONGS FROM THE DANISH]
1. The Violet—Das Veilchen   (B–G)
2. Autumn [Whither?]—Herbst   (B♭/C–A)

Date: 1900 (PW, TB).

MS: *Stichvorlagen* (?autographs) originally Harmonie-Verlag, according
to contract, now lost. MS of *Efteraar* [Autumn], signed and dated, 1952
list.

Publication: 1906, Verlag Harmonie, Berlin, in *Fünf Lieder/Five Songs*, nos.
1, 4 (pp. 2–4, 10–13), Ch. 76, Ger. and Eng. text. Cover printing reversed
out of solid olive green, Stich u. Druck: Berliner Musikalien Druckerei
GmbH Charlottenberg. The two verses of no. 1, words and music,
written out in full.

1921, Transferred to Universal Edition, 3892; a reprint of the above.

1939, transferred to Boosey & Hawkes. Later reprinted unaltered by
Boosey & Hawkes Inc. in U.S.A.

1949, Boosey & Hawkes 16557, another reprint.

1977, Boosey & Hawkes, in 20327 Song Album (with some corrections).

Words: Ludvig Holstein (1864–1943): *Digte*, Viol (first 2 of the 3 verses);
Far, hvor flyver Svanerne hen? (omitting verse 3 of the 4 verses).
Note: the Harmonie, UE and first Boosey editions attributed 'Autumn'
to J. P. Jacobsen.
Originally set to the Danish words; Eng. trans. by FD, Ger. trans. by
Jelka Delius. See also below.

Notes: TB 113; Holland 32–4, 53.
The original printing by Harmonie, as well as the first Universal issue,
gives no name for the English translator; later copies of the Universal
edition attribute the English words to Addie Funk. A letter from Jelka
Delius to Cecily Arnold, 7 November 1931, however, states: 'These
translations were really made by FD himself . . . [Listing titles of the *Fünf
Lieder*]. They are just as he made them; there are no changes.' Copies
printed after 1932 correctly attribute the Eng. words to FD.

Orchestral version: of no. 1 by FD, 1908, for Olga Wood (perf. Liverpool,
21 March; Birmingham 25 March; see HJW 312, giving incorrect year, as
1909; Olga Wood's letters to FD are all 1908). MS, Beecham Libr. list;
copy RAM (Sir Henry Wood Library). Orch: 1.1.2.2—4.0.0.0—Strings.
Full score, Boosey & Hawkes 16557, pp. 4; material, Boosey Hire
Library.

Nos. 1 and 2, orchestrated by Sir Thomas Beecham (according to concert
programme, 18 November 1946). Orch: 2.2.2.2—4.4.0.0—Harp—
Strings. MS, Beecham Libr. list. Perf: 18 November 1946, London,
Central Hall, Elsie Suddaby; no. 2 also 11 September 1931, Promenade
Concert, Dora Labette, cond. Sir Henry J. Wood.

V/22 SCHWARZE ROSEN
Black Roses

(C♭–F)

Date: Publisher's MS undated; 1901 on printed copy. (Letter from Jelka Delius to Cecily Arnold, 12 January 1933, gives 1908).

MS: Autograph, Oxford University Press, n.d. Ger. words only (partly in Jelka Delius's hand). Facsimile of a portion in DLP 34. The original publisher's proof sheets had English words written in by Jelka Delius (Travis and Emery 1974).

Publication: 1915, Tischer & Jagenberg, Cologne, 254, no. 4 of *Fünf Gesänge* (separately published), Ger. and Eng. text. (Ger. by Jelka Delius, Eng. by FD). Black and green printing on ribbed buff wrappers.

1930, Oxford University Press, London, a reprint of above.

1969, ditto, in *A Book of Songs*; set 1, re-engraved, Eng. only.

Words: Ernst Josephson (1851–1906): *Svarta Rosor och Gula,* Svarta Rosor (Paris, 1884) (setting the first two only of the three stanzas).

Notes: Holland 36, 53. FD's only setting of words originally from the Swedish. J. Sibelius's setting (of all 3 stanzas!) is his op. 36 no. 1, and dates from 1899.

Orchestrated version: by Norman Del Mar; performed 21 November 1946, London, Central Hall, Marjorie Thomas; MS, Beecham Libr. unpubl.

V/23 'JEG HØRER I NATTEN'
'Ich hör' in der Nacht'
'I hear in the night'

(B♯–G♭)

Date: 1901 (MS).

MS: Autograph, DT 36, ff 57–60 (RL 127–8), dated. Danish words, with Ger. trans. pasted over and Eng. trans. pencilled above; both the latter in the hand of Jelka Delius.

Publication: none.

Words: Holger Drachmann: *Ungdom i Digt og Sang* (1879), Sange til en Søster, 3.

Notes: not in PW.

V/24 **SUMMER LANDSCAPE**
Sommer Landschaft
Sommer i Gurre

(B♭ major; D–F)

Date: April 1902 (MS); orchestral version 1903.

MS: Autograph, DT 36 ff 61–2 (RL 128–9), dated *Frederick Delius 1902 April*, Danish words; Ger. trans. added by Jelka Delius. Also two copies in the hand of Jelka Delius (Danish/Ger./Eng. and Ger./Eng.). The original autograph differed slightly in the piano postlude; the orchestral version extended this passage, and the other MS copies above-mentioned then followed the orchestral version, or were altered to do so.

Publication: 1952, Oxford University Press, London. Eng. words only.

1969, ditto, in *A Book of Songs*, set 1, re-engraved, Eng. words only.

Words: Holger Drachmann:
'Sommer i Gurre' (1876), from *Ungdom i Digt og Sang*, Akvareller Undervejs (1879).

Notes: Holland 35, 53; not in PW.

Orchestral version: by FD, 1903. Autograph MS DT 36 ff 63–70 (RL 128), dated 1903, with a number of revisions; Danish words with Ger. and Eng. translations.
Orch: 2. 2. CA 2. 2—4. 0. 0. 0—Timp.—Harp—Strings.
Fair copy, ?Beecham Libr.
Copyist's copy and orchestral material, Oxford University Press hire library.

V/25 'THE NIGHTINGALE HAS A LYRE OF GOLD'
'Die Nachtigall spielt auf goldener Leier'

(D–G)

Date: 1910 (MS and printed copies; PW and TB give 1908).

MS: Autograph, Oxford University Press, dated 1910, Eng. words only. Original publisher's proof sheets had German translation written by Jelka Delius (Travis and Emery, 1974).

Publication: 1915, Tischer & Jagenberg, Cologne, 252, no. 2 of *Fünf Gesänge* (separately issued), Eng. and Ger. text (Ger. translator unnamed— probably Jelka Delius).

1930, Oxford University Press, a reprint of above.

1969, ditto, in *A Book of Songs*, set 2, re-engraved, Eng. words only.

Words: William Ernest Henley (1849–1903): *Life and Death (Echoes)* XVIII, (1876).

Notes: TB 169; Holland 21, 46–7.

Orchestrated version: by Norman Del Mar; performed 21 November 1946, London, Central Hall, John Kentish; MS Beecham Libr. unpubl.

V/26 LA LUNE BLANCHE

(D–F)

Date: 1910 (PW); Jelka Delius's letter to Cecily Arnold, 12 January 1933, gives 1903. But see Jelka Delius to Dr. G. Tischer, 1 August 1910: 'The third Verlaine song has already been begun'; FD ditto, 22 August 1910: *I am sending you the Verlaine song today.*

MS: Autograph unlocated; a MS on Beecham Libr. list.

Publication: 1910, Tischer & Jagenberg, Cologne, 21; no. 3 (Mondlicht) of 'Drei Lieder, Dichtungen von P. Verlaine', pp. 8–10, French and Ger. words (Ger. trans. by G. Tischer). (For nos. 1–2 see *Deux Mélodies, poésies de Paul Verlaine*, 1895, p. 109 supra). Also issued separately.

1930, Transferred to Oxford University Press.

1969, ditto, in *A Book of Songs*, set 2, re-engraved, French words only.

Words: Paul Verlaine: *La Bonne Chanson,* VI (1870).

Other settings of the poem:
by Gabriel Fauré, *La Bonne Chanson,* op. 61 no. 3, 1891–2
by Reynaldo Hahn, *Chansons Grises*, V, 'L'heure exquise', 1903.

Notes: Holland 39–40.

Orchestral version: by FD; a MS, Beecham Libr. list, unpublished. (2.2.2.2—4.0.0.0—Timp.—Solo violin & Strings). Performed 25 January 1915, London, Grafton Galleries, Jean Waterston. PW 202–3.

Date: 1911 (MS).

MS: Autograph, Oxford University Press, dated 1911, French words only. Ger. trans. originally by G. Tischer, but a different one written into Tischer's proof sheets by Jelka Delius (Travis and Emery, 1974).

Publication: 1915, Tischer & Jagenberg, Cologne, 255, no. 5 (Herbstlied) of *Fünf Gesänge* (separately issued), French and Ger. words (see above re- Ger. trans.).

1930, Transferred to Oxford University Press.

1969, ditto, in *A Book of Songs*, set 2, re-engraved, French words only.

Words: Paul Verlaine:

Poèmes saturniens (1867), Paysages tristes.

Another setting of the poem, by Reynaldo Hahn, *Chansons Grises*, I, 1903.

Notes: Holland 40–1; not in PW.

Jelka Delius, writing to Henry and Marie Clews on 23 January 1923, stated 'Binding the Poet has translated a Verlaine song most admirably'.

Date: 1913 (copy MS).

MS: Autograph unlocated; copy in the hand of Jelka Delius, Oxford University Press, dated 1913, Eng. words only. Original publisher's proof sheets had Ger. trans. written in by Jelka Delius (Travis and Emery, 1974) (see below also).

Publication: 1915, Tischer & Jagenberg, Cologne, 253, no. 3 of *Fünf Gesänge* (separately issued), Eng. and Ger. words (see above re Ger. trans).

1930, Transferred to Oxford University Press.

1969, ditto, in *A Book of Songs*, set 1, re-engraved, Eng. words only.

Words: 'Fiona Macleod' [William Sharp] (1856–1905): *The Hour of Beauty*.

Notes: PW 155 (134–5); TB 169; Holland 21, 47–8, 54.

Orchestral version: (by FD?); MS, Beecham Libr. list, unpubl.
Orch: 2.2. CA. 2.2.—Strings.
Performed 21 November 1946, London, Central Hall, Marjorie Thomas (programme attributes orchestral version to FD). In the proof sheets, with Travis and Emery in 1974, pencilled notes on orchestration, in FD's hand, subsequently rubbed out, could still just be discerned.

Note: Probably dating from this time or a little later are the incomplete sketches (first stanza and first line of second stanza only, of the 3 stanzas) of a song setting *The Lake Isle of Innisfree*, from *The Rose* (1893) by William Butler Yeats (1865–1939). These are to be found in the 'larger small sketch book' now in the Grainger Museum; see Appendix and SM7, 74.

V/29 TWO SONGS FOR CHILDREN
[for chorus with pianoforte accompaniment]
1. Little Birdie ['What does little birdie say?'] (unison)
2. The Streamlet's Slumber Song (two-part)

Date: 1913 (letter FD to Silver, Burdett).

MS: (*a*). Autograph pencil drafts, DT 39 ff 82a, 81b (RL 145).

    (*b*). Last page of MS of no. 2, Beecham Libr. list (?same as *a*).

    (*c*). Autograph fair copy unlocated; ?sent to American publisher, v. inf.

    (*d*). Copy in the hand of Jelka Delius, prepared in 1923 for Oxford University Press, but at present unlocated.

Publication: c. 1916, (acc. to Library of Congress); Silver, Burdett & Co., New Jersey, USA, *Progressive Music Series*, Bk 2, 'Composed for this series'. [?item 1 only].
[1924] (n.d. but BL accession date 12 May 1924), Oxford University Press, included in: The Oxford Choral Songs, nos. 22 and 115, with Tonic Sol-fa. Later copies (no. 1 copyright 1934, no. 2 1942) bear a footnote referring to the American first edition.

Words: 1. Tennyson; *Sea Dreams*, 1860. 2 verses, strophic.
    2. ?[unattributed] 2 verses, strophic

Notes: PW 170 (210).

V/30 FOUR OLD ENGLISH LYRICS
[Four Elizabethan Songs]
Vier altenglische Lieder

	(orig: high) (transposed: low)
1. It was a lover and his lass	(C♯–A; A–F)
2. So white, so soft, so sweet is she	(B–F♯; G♯–D♯)
3. Spring, the sweet Spring	(D–A; B♭–F)
4. To Daffodils	(C♯–G♯; A♯–E)

Dates: 1. 1916 (PW)
2. March 1915
3. February 1915 } (printed copies)
4. March 1915

MS: Autographs ?formerly Winthrop Rogers Ltd. MSS of nos. 2, 3 & 4 appear on the Beecham Libr. list. A MS copy of no. 3, in Philip Heseltine's hand, with notes on projected orchestration, bought by R. Macnutt at Sothebys, 16 December 1964 (item 401). (This shows a slightly different reading in the last bar).

Publication: 1919, Winthrop Rogers Ltd., London; nos. —, 4013/2, —, 4002; Eng. words only. Issued separately only; and issued in high (orig.) and low (transposed) keys. Reprinted by Boosey & Hawkes.

[?1919], Universal Edition, Vienna, 6919–6922 a/b; an entirely different engraving from the Winthrop Rogers one. Ger. and Eng. words (for translations, see below). High and low keys.

1977, Boosey & Hawkes, in 20327 Song album (with some corrections).

Words: 1. Shakespeare (1564–1616), *As you like it*, V, iii. (omitting the third of the 4 stanzas).
2. Ben Jonson (1572–1637), *Underwoods* (1640), A Celebration of Charis, iv. Her Triumph. (The last of the 3 stanzas only.)
3. Thomas Nashe (1567–1601), Spring. (Ver's song from *Summer's Last Will and Testament* (1600).)
4. Robert Herrick (1591–1674), *Hesperides* (1648), To Daffodils.

Translations (for Universal Edition publication):
1. Mit ihrem Liebsten ging die Maid (later copies: War einst ein Liebster und sein Schatz), trans. Alice Blau.
2. So weiss, so sanft [zart], so süss, trans. Margarethe Gottlieb.
3. Lieblicher Mai (later copies: Mai, süsser Mai).
4. Narzissen, trans. Margarethe Gottlieb.

Notes: TB 174; Holland 21–2, 48–51, 54.

Orchestrated versions: 1. None, as far as known.
2. by Peter Warlock (Philip Heseltine). MS, in the hand of Philip Heseltine, coll. O. W. Neighbour; pp. 5, dated October 1926. Orch: 2. 1. 2. 2—1. 0. 0. 0—Strings. Unpubl. This version is transposed up one whole tone above the published high key version.
3. 'by or for Sir Thomas Beecham' (Holland, 54). MS, Beecham Libr. list. Orch: 2. 2. CA. 2. 2—1. 0. 0. 0—Strings. Unpubl. (See also under MS above).

4. by Norman Del Mar, performed 21 November 1946, London, Central Hall, John Kentish. MS, Beecham Libr. list. Unpubl..

The slight discrepancy between the high and low versions of no. 2 in the third bar from the end is not resolved by Warlock's orchestral version; which (despite its extra high key) follows the harmonic spacing of the low version.

Plate 16: Sketch for early version of song: *Avant que tu ne t'en ailles*

V/31 **AVANT QUE TU NE T'EN AILLES**

(D♯–A)

Date: 1919 (PW, TB); completed and published 1932.

MS: (*a*). Autograph sketch of *first* version, incomplete, DT 36 f 70 (RL 128), n.d. French words only, *see plate 16*.

(*b*). Autograph sketches and draft of final version, incomplete, Grainger Museum, Melbourne, Australia, pp. 2, n.d. French words only. See SM7 71–2.

(*c*). *Stichvorlage* in the hand of Eric Fenby, with French words interlined in the hand of Jelka Delius, Boosey & Hawkes archives, n.d., pp. 4.

Publication: 1932, Boosey & Hawkes 7101, French words only.

1968, Boosey & Hawkes 19607, re-engraved, with Eng. trans. by John Andrewes ('Morning Star') added.

1977, the latter included in Boosey & Hawkes 20327 Song Album.

Words: Paul Verlaine:
La Bonne Chanson, V (1870).

Notes: TB 182; Holland 41.

Five bars of the Eric Fenby/Jelka Delius MS reproduced in the *Daily Telegraph*, 23 January 1932, p. 13, illustrating Herbert Hughes' article: 'New compositions by Delius—"Fantastic Dance" and a setting of Verlaine'.

VI Works for orchestra alone:

VI/1 FLORIDA

[MS.]

Tropische Scenen für Orchester

[Printed score]

Suite for Orchestra

1. Tages Anbruch	Daybreak
2. Am Fluss	By the River
3. Sonnenuntergang—Bei der Plantage	Sunset
4. Nachts	At Night

(1: A min/maj—D maj; 2: E♭ maj; 3: orig. D min/maj; rev. E min—A maj; 4: A min—D maj).

Date: 1887 on orig. MS; 1886–7 (PW). In 1889 two movements (unspecified) were revised, of which only 'Le coucher du Soleil—Pastorale (tiré de la suite Florida)', numbered II, survives.

Dedication: 'Dedicated to the People of Florida' (on published score, but not on MSS).

Orchestra: *Original version:*
(i) Picc. 2. 2. 2. 2—4. 2. 3. 1—Timp. Cym. Tbno. Trgl.—Harp—Strings.
(ii) Picc. 1. 2. 2. 2—4. 0. 0. 0—Timp.—Harp—Strings.
(iii) 2. 2. 2. 2—4. 2. 3. 1—Timp. Cym.—Harp—Strings.
(iv) 2. 1. 2. 2—4. 1. 1. 0—Timp.—Harp—Strings.
Revised version:
(iii) Picc. 2. 2. CA. 2. BsCl. 2—4. 2. 3. 1—Timp. BD. Cym. Tbno. Trgl.—Harp—Strings.

MS: (*a*). Autograph full score, original version, Grainger Museum, Melbourne, Australia, pp. 102, oblong format, dated *Fritz Delius 1887*. Now defective, pp. 57–82 (comprising the entire third movement except for the first and last pages thereof) having been removed. Some performing marks added by Beecham.

(*b*). Autograph full score, revised version, third movement only, Grainger Museum, pp. 34, n.d. but signed. Headed "II" (see above).

(*c*). Copy of the 'Calinda' (i.e. second section of the first movement) in the hand of Eric Fenby, dated 1887 (!), Boosey & Hawkes archives. (This MS cuts from 3 bars after cue 11 to cue 14 of the published score).

(*d*). Copy, movements 1, 2 & 4 original version and 3 revised version, in the hand of George Brownfoot, ?Beecham library. (This score was used as the basis for engraving the work for publication).

Publication: 1963, Boosey & Hawkes, full score 18482 and miniature score HPS 748, pp. 114; in 'Complete Works. Revised and Edited by the late Sir Thomas Beecham, Bart.' Issued as '(Op. posth.)'
This score comprises movements 1, 2 & 4 of the original version and movement 3 of the revised version. Facsimile of 4 pp. from MS of movement 3, GC 32–5.

Performance: early 1888—Leipzig, restaurant Rosenthal, cond. Hans Sitt (private performance).

1 April 1937—London, Queen's Hall, LPO, Beecham (omitting the second movement).

October 1959—BBC Third programme, RPO, Beecham (complete).

Notes: PW 27 (47); TB 36–8, 40, 52; SM7 69–71.

The opening theme of movements 1 & 4 is used in the opera *The Magic Fountain;* so are the dance at the climax of movement 3 and some other themes from that movement. The second section of the first movement—the Calinda dance—is used prominently in Act II of the opera *Koanga.*

FD to Grieg, n.d. [early June 1889] . . . *reworking my Florida Suite & I have finished two of the chief movements.*

The 3 short cuts marked by Beecham in the published score (first movement) were observed by him in performance and recording.

VI/2 HIAWATHA
ein Tongedicht für Orchester
nach Longfellows Gedicht

Date: 1888 January (MS). Commenced late 1887 (TB).

Dedication: none.

Orchestra: 3. 2. 2. 2—4. 2. 3 Tenors. 1—Timp. Trgl. Tamt.—Harp—Strings.

MS: Autograph full score, DT 1 (RL 16–19), pp. 90, dated *Fritz Delius 1888 Januar*. Now defective; pp. 4–17 and 46–53 missing.

Publication: none. Facsimile of first page of MS score, RL 16. A 4-bar excerpt (in piano arrangement), GC 40.

Performance: none as far as known.

Notes: TB 36–7; EF 68. The excerpt quoted in GC 40 shows the earliest form of the viola melody, later heard in *Paris*. Quotations from Longfellow's poem appear beside the music in the MS score, v. RL loc. cit.

VI/3 RHAPSODISCHE VARIATIONEN
für grosses Orchester

Date: *St. Malo. September 1888.*

Orchestra: Picc. 2. 2. 2. 3—4. 2. 2 Cornets. 3. 1—Timp. BD. Cym. Trgl.—Strings.

MS: Autograph full score, unfinished, DT 3 ff 52–68 (RL 25), pp. 32, dated.

Publication: } none.
Performance:

VI/4 [THREE PIECES for String Orchestra]

Date: 1888 (v. inf.).

MS: lost? On Beecham Libr. list appears 'MS score of a piece for strings, 1888.'

Publication: } none
Performance: }

Notes: FD to Grieg from St. Malo, n.d. but probably October, 1888: *I have also written 3 pieces for string orchestra.* LKC 17–18.

VI/5 IDYLLE DE PRINTEMPS

Date: 1889 (MS).

Orchestra: (? details).

MS: Autograph full score, Beecham Libr. list.

Publication: } none
Performance: }

Notes: no further information available.

VI/6 SUITE D'ORCHESTRE

1. Marche [Caprice]   (C major)
2. La Quadroone (Rapsodie Floridienne)
3. Berceuse
4. Scherzo
5. Thème et Variations

Date: 1889–90 (MSS). Item 1, 1890, a revised version of *Marche Caprice*,
1888 (PW 160; TB 52); item 2, 1889; item 4, 1890 (according to Beecham
Libr. list).

Orchestra: of item 1 as published:
2. 2. 2. 2—4. 2. 3 (2 Tenor, 1 Bass). 1—Timp. BD. Cym. Trgl. SD—
Strings.

MS: Autograph full scores of items 2 and 4 (and formerly 1 also) Beecham
Libr. list. A *Marche Française*, full score dated 1890, appears on the same
list. As only items 1, 2 and 4 are shown on the 1935 and 1952 lists, the
survival of items 3 and 5 seems doubtful.

Publication: item 1 only, *Marche Caprice*:
1951, Joseph Williams, full score 5812 and miniature score, no. 2, pp. 22,
'Edited and Arranged by Sir Thomas Beecham'.
items 2–5: unpublished.

Performance: item 1 only: 21 November 1946, London, Central Hall
Westminster, RPO, Beecham.

Notes: TB 37, 52. PW 160 (198) does not include item 2. In a letter to Grieg,
n.d. but probably early June 1889, FD lists the movements as *Marche,
Berceuse, Scherzo, Duo & Theme with Variations*.

The autograph pencil draft score of a *Marche des Marionettes*, n.d. but
apparently of this period, is now bound into DT 39 ff 14–17 (RL 135),
pp. 7. Unpublished.
Orchestra. 2. 2. 2. 2—4. 2. 3. 1—Timp.—Strings.

VI/7 **3 SYMPHONISCHE DICHTUNGEN**
(Three Small Tone Poems)
1. Sommer Abend   Summer Evening
2. Winter Nacht [Schlittenfahrt]   Winter Night [Sleigh Ride]
3. Frühlings Morgen   Spring Morning

   (1 : D maj; 2: A maj; 3: A maj.)

Date: 1890 (MS). Item 2, 1888 according to PW 160 (200), TB 36.

Orchestra: of item 1 as published:
   3. 2. 2. 2—4. 2. 3 (2 Tenor, 1 Bass). 1—Timp.—Strings
   of item 2: Picc. 2. 2. 2. 2—4. 2. 2 Cornets. 3. 1—Timp. Schellen. Cym.—
   Strings
   of item 3:?

MS: (*a*). Autograph full scores, Beecham Libr. list.

   (*b*). Copy of item 2 in the hand of George Brownfoot, DT 49 (RL 163),
   pp. 39.

Publication: item 1: *Summer Evening:*
   1951, Joseph Williams, full score 5813 and miniature score, no. 3, pp. 20.
   'Edited and Arranged by Sir Thomas Beecham.'

   item 2: *Winter Night (Sleigh Ride).*
   1976, Boosey & Hawkes, full score 20346, pp. 21. Material on hire.
   item 3: none.

Arrangements: item 2 only:
   1967, The Sacred Music Press, Dayton, Ohio, USA, 'arranged for organ
   by Robert Hebble', in 'Ted Alan Worth in Concert', pp. 4–11.

   1969, for piano solo by Robert Threlfall, MS arranger. To be included
   in an Album of piano solos by FD (original and arrangements) in hand
   (1977) for publication by Boosey & Hawkes.

Performance: items 1, 2 and 3, 18 November 1946, London, Central Hall,
   Westminster, RPO, Richard Austin.

Notes: TB 36, 60; PW 27 (46), (188), 160 (198).
   Item 2—Winter Night—is apparently an orchestral version of the
   Norwegische Schlittenfahrt (Norwegian Sleigh Ride) played to Grieg and
   Sinding as a piano piece (q.v.) on Christmas Eve 1887.

According to Felix Aprahamian's programme note for the first
performance, the following lines (here translated from the German) were
prefixed to *Winter Night:*
*One Christmas eve I stood in the open air. The moon shone bright over the
billowing landscape. The sound of an approaching sleigh was heard from a
distance, but it soon rushed by and disappeared. And then gradually it was
once more still and bright and peaceful.*

A work entitled *Autumn (Tone Poem)* was also in the possession of Sir
Thomas Beecham, though not appearing on the Beecham Libr. list:
could it have been a fourth 'seasonal' item to the other three above listed?

VI/8 [portion of an orchestral work, the surviving section headed:
A L'AMORE]

Date: ?1890. Paper and style of writing closely resemble the MS of the
Légendes (Sagen) pour piano & orchestre, dated that year.

Orchestra: 3. 2. CA. 2. 2—4. 2. 3. 1—Harp—Strings.

MS: Autograph pencil draft score, DT 39 ff 19–23 (RL 138), pp. 46–55, n.d.
The movement in B major headed *A l'Amore* begins on p. 47, but is
incomplete.

Publication: none.

VI/9 **PETITE SUITE D'ORCHESTRE**
1. Allegro ma non troppo (G minor)
2. Con moto   (G minor)
3. Allegretto   (E major)

Date: 1890 (MS).

Orchestra: 2. 2. 2. 2—2. 1. 0. 0—Timp.—Strings.

MS: (*a*). Autograph full score, DT 48a. ff 1–12 (RL 160–2), pp. 22, dated
1890.

(*b*). Copy in the hand of William Borner, DT 48b. ff 13–24 (RL ibid.),
pp. 22.

Publication: none. Facsimile of first page of MS score, RL 160.

Performance: none.

Notes: TB 60; not in PW. Beecham refers to the 'short suite in two
movements for small orchestra.' The widely different key of the third
movement notwithstanding, the original MS is clearly one sequence of
pieces.

VI/10 PAA VIDDERNE
(Auf dem Hochgebirg)

Symphonische Dichtung nach dem Gedicht von Henrik Ibsen.
Sur les cimes: Poème symphonique d'après une poésie de H. I.
On the Mountains: Symphonic poem after H. I's Paa Vidderne.

(E major)

Date: 1890–2. A letter from Grieg to FD of 22 December 1890 refers to the work; the MS is dated 1892.

Orchestra: Picc. 2. 2. 2. BsCl. 2—4. 2. 2 Cornets. 3 (Tenors). 1—Timp. Trgl. Cym.—Harp—Strings.

MS: (*a*). Autograph full score, DT 5a. ff 1–30 (RL 32–36), pp. 55, dated *Fritz Delius 1892*, and showing signs of revision, v. Rachel Lowe inf.

(*b*). Copy in the hand of an unidentified copyist, DT 5b. ff 31–56 (RL 36), pp. 51. This copy has Sir Thomas Beecham's performing marks in blue pencil.

Publication: none. Facsimile of first page of MS score, RL 32.

Performance: 10 October 1891, Oslo, Christiania Music Society, Iver Holter. ('Concertouverture').

25 February 1894, Monte Carlo, M. Steck.

8 November 1946, London, Albert Hall, RPO, Beecham.

Notes: PW 36 (53), (188); TB 63.
The last 5 lines of Ibsen's poem appear on the titlepage in Ger. trans. On the last page of the score, a motif already noted in the melodrama of the same title is heard. (v. p. 73 above.)
See also: Rachel Lowe, 'Delius's First Performance,' *Musical Times* (March 1965), pp. 190–2; 'Delius and Norway' *Studies in Music* (6/1972; 7/1973) (reprinted in *A Delius Companion*, pp. 167 sqq.)

VI/11 **OVER THE HILLS AND FAR AWAY**
Über die Berge in die Ferne
Fantasia [Fantasie Ouverture]

(C major)

Date: 1893 (Chop); 1895 (PW); 1897 (copy MS, v. inf.); finished 1897 (TB 93).

Orchestra: 3. 2. 2. 3—4. 2. 3 (Tenors). 1—Timp. Cym. SD—Strings.

MS: (*a*). The autograph full score remains at present untraced.

(*b*). Copy in the hand of an unidentified copyist, DT 9 ff 1–14 (RL 43–4), pp. 26, n.d. This MS is 60 bars shorter than the final version, despite an added leaf in FD's own hand, and some alterations to detail likewise.

(*c*). Copy in the hand of the 'Paris copyist', DT 9 ff 15–43 (RL 44), pp. 55, n.d. This MS agrees in essence with the published score; as do the following ones.

(*d*). Copy in the hand of Eric Fenby, Memorial Library of Music, Stanford University, California, pp. 38, dated 1897.

(*e*). Copy in the hand of Eric Fenby, DT 9B/1, pp. [34], n.d.

Publication: 1950, G. Schirmer Inc., New York, full score 42422, pp. 46. 'Miscellany, No. 174.' 'Edited by Sir Thomas Beecham.'

Performance: 13 November 1897, Elberfeld, Elberfelder Konzert-Gesellschaft, Hans Haym.

30 May 1899, London, St. James's Hall, Alfred Hertz.

16 May 1908, London, Queen's Hall, New Symphony Orchestra, Thomas Beecham.

Notes: PW 40 (55); TB 93–4, 97–8; Chop 18, item 2.
A motif already noted in both works entitled *Paa Vidderne* (q.v.) also occurs in this work, cf. bars 74–5 etc.
Beecham, in his recording of this work, cut bars 183–192 inclusive.
For use of the score in a ballet, see under *A Village Romeo and Juliet* above.

VI/12 **APPALACHIA**
American Rhapsody for Orchestra

Date: 1896 (MS).

Orchestra: Picc. 2. 2. 2. 3—4. 2. 2 Cornets à piston. 3 (Tenors). 1—Timp. BD. Cym. Trgl. SD—2 Harps—Strings.

MS: Autograph full score DT 9 ff 44–72 (RL 46–49) pp. 29, dated *Fritz Delius 1896*.
Now defective; wanting p. 15.

Publication: none. Facsimiles of pp. 1 and 16, RL 46, 48; of pp. 8 and 17, plates 17–18.

Performance: none.

Notes: TB 73, 100.
Apart from some material in common with the great choral work of the same title of 1902, *Yankee Doodle* and *Dixie* are also introduced. Christopher Palmer having identified the references to those two popular tunes for me, two further pages of the MS are here reproduced in facsimile: p. 8 showing the introduction of the 'Appalachia' melody in sprightly tempo, p. 17 the addition thereto of 'Dixie' as a counterpoint (followed a few bars later, on the next page—not reproduced here—by 'Yankee Doodle' likewise), *see plates 17 and 18.*

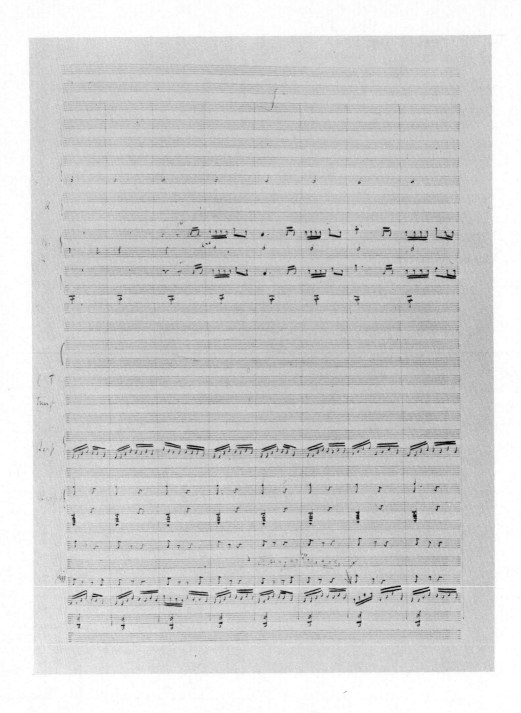

Plates 17–18: Appalachia. American Rhapsody, pages 8 and 17

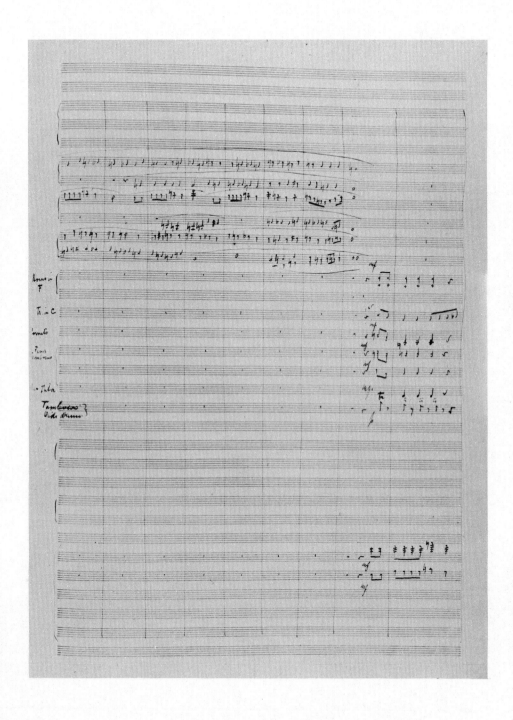

Plate 18

135

VI/13 LA RONDE SE DÉROULE
Symphonische Dichtung zu 'Dansen Gaar'
Drama von Helge Rode

Date: 1899 (MS); 1898 (Chop).

Orchestra: 3. Picc. 3. 3. BsCl. 3. Contra—4. 3. 3 (Tenors). 1—Timp. *zum Schluss ein zweiter Paukenspieler*, BD. Cym. Trgl.—Harp—Strings.

MS: Autograph full score DT 15 ff 1–42 (RL 68–9), pp. 40, dated *Fritz Delius 1899*.

Publication: none, in this form. Facsimile of last page of MS score, RL 68. See *Lebenstanz* (Life's Dance), 1901–1912 inf.

Performance: 30 May 1899, London, St. James's Hall, Alfred Hertz.

Notes: PW 42 (57), 45 (59), 152 (132); TB 100; Chop 19, item 6.
Nine lines of Helge Rode's play appear on the titlepage of this MS. This is the first version of the work later entitled *Lebenstanz* (Life's Dance). The essential thematic material is all to be found in this earlier version, which however lacks the more elaborate development and transformation of themes of the final version; the latter also differs in the basic key-sequence of the subsidiary themes.

VI/14 PARIS
Ein Nachtstück (The Song of a great City)
für grosses Orchester

Date: 1899 (published score).

Dedication: 'Dr. Hans Haym gewidmet'.

Orchestra: Picc. 2. 3. CA. 3. BsCl. 3. Contra—6. 3. 3 (Tenors). 1—Timp. BD. Cym. Trgl. Tamt. Tbno. Castanets. Glockenspiel—2 Harps— Strings: 16. 16. 12. 12. 12.

MS: (*a*). The autograph full score is untraced at present. Whether it formed Leuckart's *Stichvorlage* or not is unknown.

(*b*). A MS (?copy) was listed in the 1935 and 1952 lists as 'Paris, full score, 1899–1900' and included in the Beecham Libr. list.

(*c*). Sketches, in full and short score, DT 40 ff 1–29 (RL 150–1), n.d. These fall into two originally separate groups: *Scènes Parisiennes* and *Episodes et Aventures*, v. also TB 84. Facsimiles of portion in DLP 44.

Publication: 1909, F. E. C. Leuckart, Leipzig, full score 6320, lithographed. (Autographie und Druck Röder), pp. 66.

1921, Transferred to Universal Edition catalogue, full score 6900; study score later issued, 7018, reduced from above.

1965, Universal Edition, full score 6900, pp. 76, engraved; study score ditto 13874. Corrected, and incorporating a number of details (bowing, etc.) from a Beecham-marked score now in the DT archive.

Performance: 14 December 1901, Elberfeld, Elberfelder Konzertgesellschaft, Hans Haym

15 November 1902, Berlin, Philharmonic Orchestra, Beethoven-Saal, Ferruccio Busoni

12 February 1903, Düsseldorf, Julius Buths

24 October 1904, Elberfeld, Hans Haym

3 December 1905, Brussels, Concerts Populaires, Sylvain Dupuis

11 January 1908, Liverpool, Philharmonic Hall, New Symphony Orchestra, Thomas Beecham

26 February 1908, London, Queen's Hall, New Symphony Orchestra, Thomas Beecham

26 November 1909, Boston, Symphony Orchestra, Max Fiedler

Arrangements: For two pianos by Julius Buths (*Paris*—Impressions de nuit); MS DT 18a/b (RL 74–5), n.d. but probably 1903 (v. Buths to FD 24 June 1903). Unpubl.

This arrangement reveals an earlier state of the work, in some details, than the published score of 1909. Buths to FD, September 1903: 'I have not written the alterations in question into the score but will see if I can do so.'

Notes: PW 131 (117–8); TB 94, 149; MC 64; EF 193; Chop 19, item 7.
See also: Bernard Shore: *The Orchestra speaks*, Longmans, Green (London 1938), pp. 42–6.

Felix Aprahamian's programme note for the performance at the second Delius Festival, on 4 November 1946, quotes the following lines as prefixed to the original score:

Mysterious city—
City of pleasures,
Of gay music and dancing,
Of painted and beautiful women—
Wondrous city
Unveiling but to those who,
Shunning day,
Live through the night
And return home
To the sound of awakening streets
And the rising dawn.

French phrases in draft for this are to be found in the sketches for the work in DT 40, f 3.

The music of *Paris* was used (complete) for a ballet entitled 'Nocturne' by [Sir] Frederick Ashton, Sadlers Wells Ballet, London, Sadlers Wells, 10 November 1936 (Frederick Ashton, Margot Fonteyn, Robert Helpmann).

A copy of the printed score, very fully annotated by Sir Thomas Beecham, is in the DT Archive.

VI/15 LEBENSTANZ
Life's Dance—Ronde de la vie
[a tone poem]—(1901 MS)
für grosses Orchester

Date: 1901 (MS); final version 1912 (MS).

Dedication: 'Oskar Fried gewidmet' (final version).

Orchestra: 3. Picc. 3. CA. 3. BsCl. 3. Contra—4. 3. 3 (Tenors). 1—Timp.
BD. Cym. Trgl. (SD in 1901 score only). Glockenspiel—Harp(s)—Strings.

MS: (*a*). Autograph full score, DT 16 ff 1–27/28 (RL 70), pp. 54, dated
1901 Frederick Delius.

(*b*). Copy, principally in the hand of the 'Paris copyist', but with a
different ending in FD's own hand now added, DT 17 ff 1–42 (RL 71–3),
pp. 81, dated *Frederick Delius . . . 1912*. The original French instrument
titles—violons, altos, etc.—altered to English and Italian. This MS was
apparently used for the engraving.

Publication: 1912, Tischer & Jagenberg, Cologne, full score 155, pp. 63.
1930, transferred to Oxford University Press.

Performance: 21 January 1904, Düsseldorf, Julius Buths
24 October 1904, Elberfeld, Hans Haym
19 January 1908, London, Albert Hall, LSO, E. F. Arbos — *Chicago. 7 Nov 1912*
15 November 1912, Berlin, Philharmonic Orchestra, Oskar Fried (final
[published] version).
25 February 1913, London, Queen's Hall, New Symphony Orchestra,
H. Balfour Gardiner.

Arrangements: For two pianos by Hans Haym, 1903, untraced.
For piano solo by Philip Heseltine, 1912, MS coll. R. Threlfall, pp. 18,
unpubl. Pencil annotations in Heseltine's hand draw attention to
similarities with motifs in *The Magic Fountain, Songs of Sunset, Song of
the High Hills* and *A Mass of Life*. Facsimile of opening in DLP 68, of
page 10 in Tomlinson, *Warlock and Delius*.

Notes: PW 51, 60 (63, 69); TB 131–2.

VI/16 **BRIGG FAIR**
An English Rhapsody

Date: 1907 (MS and published score).

Dedication: 'For Percy Grainger'.

Orchestra: 3. 2. CA. 3. BsCl. 3. Contra—6. 3. 3 (Tenors). 1—3 Timp. BD.
Trgl. 3 Tubular Bells—1 Harp (or more)—Strings: 16. 16. 12. 12. 12.
Copyist's MS wind score, reduced to double woodwind and 4 horns,
Boosey archives.

MS: (*a*). Autograph full score, dated 1907; included on 1935 list, also on
1952 list; present whereabouts untraced.

(*b*). 'Copy MS with numerous deletions' listed on 1952 list: this may have
been Leuckart's *Stichvorlage* (which, although according to the contract
it was retained by them, is now unlocated).

(*c*). 4 pages of early 2-stave sketches, coll. O. W. Neighbour. (Opening
reproduced in facsimile, DLP 60).

Publication: 1910, F. E. C. Leuckart, Leipzig, full and study scores, 6511,
pp. 39.
1921, Transferred to Universal Edition catalogue, full score 6902, study
score 6904.
—Re-engraved for miniature score, W. Phil. V. 207, pp. 48, with portrait
(1901, R. profile) (omitted in post-War reprints), introduction and
synopsis of form by E(rwin) St(ein).
1953, Re-engraved for 'Complete Works. Revised and Edited by Sir '
Thomas Beecham, Bart.', Boosey & Hawkes Inc., New York, full score
8885, pp. 43.
Note: in the USA, this work is handled by Boosey & Hawkes Inc.

Performance: 18 January 1908, Liverpool Orchestral Society, Granville
Bantock.

19 February 1908, Birmingham Town Hall, Hallé Orchestra, Landon
Ronald.

31 March 1908, London, Queen's Hall, New Symphony Orchestra,
Thomas Beecham.

28 May 1910, Zurich, Grosser Tonhallesaal, Volkmar Andreae.

28 October 1910, New York, Symphony Orchestra, Walter Damrosch.

The claim that the première was given by Suter at Basle in 1907, see PW
168–9 (206–7)—also programme note to opening concert of the 1929
Festival—was immediately contradicted in PW 51 (63) and 63 (71), and
is not supported by the correspondence between FD and Hermann Suter.

Arrangements: For piano duet, by Dagmar Juhl, 1911. Published by F.E.C.
Leuckart, 6720, pp. 19; later by Universal Edition, 6905.
For two pianos (4 hands), by Philip Heseltine, 1911; MS BL Add. 57966
ff 7–17, unpublished.
For piano solo, by Alan Rowlands; MS, arranger, unpublished.

Notes: PW 127–9 (115–6); TB 166. See also: Ernest Newman, review in *Birmingham Daily Post*, 20 February 1908.

The score is prefaced by the words of six verses of the folk-song 'Brigg Fair', in the original and in a Ger. trans. by Jelka Rosen (omitted in Beecham's edition).

Percy Grainger's setting of the folk-song, for voices unaccompanied, was published by Forsyth in 1906 (being later re-issued by Schott & Co. Ltd.). Grainger's final setting has only 5 verses (the third of FD's six not occurring) and of these, only the first 2 appear to belong to the original tune.

In the MS 2-stave sketch, at the entry of the theme, the note occurs: *Chorus (to be sung at end)*. This sketch also establishes at once, though in primitive form, the idea of the introduction. Eric Fenby, in a record sleeve-note, states '. . . like most of his works written before 1910 he revised it after the first performance notably in the introduction.'

See also: FD letter to Bantock, 1 February 1908: *I want to make a slight alteration in the score* . . . The passage he refers to, *8 bars before the $\frac{3}{2}$ at the end*, and quotes in his letter, see facsimile in GC 80–1, is unclear on comparison with the printed score at this point—possibly because of subsequent further revision. FD to Bantock, n.d. [Jan 1908]: *I tried the bells at B*[reitkopf] *& H*[ärtel]'*s this morning and they are fine.*

A copy of the printed full score marked by Sir Thomas Beecham is in the DT Archive.

For use of this work in a ballet, see under *A Village Romeo & Juliet* above.

VI/17 **IN A SUMMER GARDEN**
In einem Sommergarten
[Rhapsody for full Orchestra]—(orig. MS only)

Date: Spring 1908 (orig. MS). Revised after first performance, before
  publication.

Dedication: 'Dedicated to my wife Jelka-Rosen'.

Orchestra: 3. 2. CA. 2. BsCl. 3—4. 2. 3 (Tenors). 1—3 Timp. Glockenspiel.
  Trgl. [not in original version] [3 Tubular Bells—in original version
  only]—1 Harp (or more)—Strings: 16. 16. 12. 12. 12.

MS: *Original version:*
  (*a*). Autograph full score, DT 23 ff 1–24 (RL 85–6) pp. 42, dated *Spring
  1908*. Many pencilled overworkings, pointing towards the ultimate
  revised version.

  (*b*). Copy in the hand of Henry Gibson, made in 1942 from the (?original)
  orchestral parts, BBC Music Library.

  Revised version:
  (*c*). *Stichvorlage*, previously with Leuckart (according to the contract),
  now lost.

Publication: *Original version:*
  None. Facsimile of opening, DLP 64; facsimile of last page of MS score,
  RL 86.

  Revised version:
  1911, F. E. C. Leuckart, Leipzig, full and study scores, 6678, pp. 34.

  1921, Transferred to Universal Edition catalogue, full score 6909, large
  study score 6911.

  1964, Universal Edition, miniature score 13873 (a further reduced version
  of the original printing).
  Note: in the USA, this work is handled by Boosey & Hawkes Inc.

Performance: *Original version:*
  11 December 1908, London, Queen's Hall, orchestra of the Philharmonic
  Society, cond. F. Delius.

  Revised version:
  19 April 1912, Boston, Symphony Orchestra, Max Fiedler

  3 June 1913, Jena, ADM, Fritz Stein.

  4 November 1913, Berlin, Philharmonic Orchestra, Th. Spiering.

  18 December 1913, Edinburgh, Scottish Orchestra, E. Mlynarski.

  27 March 1914, London, Queen's Hall Orchestra, Geoffrey Toye.

Arrangements: For piano duet, by Philip Heseltine (1912–13), n.d., MS coll.
  R. Threlfall, pp. 25 [26], unpublished. (This MS now lacks the original
  outer sheet, i.e. the first page of *secundo* and last page of *primo*; the
  missing music has been reconstructed by the present owner). *See plates
  19 and 20.*

NY
26 Jan 1912

142

For piano solo, by Philip Heseltine, 1921 (?published by Universal according to some 'Warlock' literature, but disclaimed by that firm); fragmentary MS, BL Add. 57966 ff 18–19 (portion of the 6/4 section and cues 16–18 only). Other arrangements by Ph. H., proposed or completed, see Gray 42, 43, 45, 243; I. A. Copley 'Warlock and Delius—a Catalogue', *Music and Letters* July 1968.

For piano solo, by Alan Rowlands; MS arranger, unpublished.

The music of *In a Summer Garden* was used (complete), preceded by the score of *Summer Night on the River*, for a ballet of the same name by Robert Hynd; performed by the Royal Ballet (New Group), London, Sadlers Wells, 26 October 1972 (Vyvyan Lorrayne, Barry McGrath). An arrangement of the music for piano solo, for rehearsal, was made by R. Temple Savage.

Notes: PW 62 (71), 130 (117); TB 167.

The printed score is prefaced, below the dedication, with lines from Rossetti (*House of Life*—Youth and Change, part I, Sonnet LIX, 9–10). Below this again, in the Universal score only, appear the following unattributed lines:

Rosen, Lilien und tausend duftende Blumen. Bunte Schmetterlinge flattern von Kelch zu Kelch und goldbraune Bienen summen in der warmen zitternden Sommerluft. Unter schattigen alten Bäumen ein stiller Fluss mit weissen Wasserrosen. Im Kahn, fast verborgen, zwei Menschen. Eine Drossel singt—ein Unkenton in der Ferne.

(These lines appeared as the sole programme note to the June 1913 performance at the ADM).

The original and final versions differ extensively in detail and also in overall plan. In the first version, the movement in the central section was in crotchets instead of in quavers; the following passage was considerably more extended, and reminiscences of the opening phrase (on horn and oboe solo) and of the central section came before the coda.

A copy of the printed full score very fully marked by Sir Thos. Beecham is in the DT Archive.

Plates 19–20: In a Summer Garden, arrangement for piano duet by Philip
Heseltine, pages 17–18

Plate 20

VI/18 **A DANCE RHAPSODY [No. 1]**
Tanzrhapsodie

Date: 1908 (printed score). Letters of FD to Bantock, 17 February and 24 April 1909, refer to the recent finish of the work.

Dedication: 'Hermann Suter gewidmet'.

Orchestra: 3 (incl. Picc). 1. CA. BsOb. 3. BsCl. 3. Sarrus (Contra)—6. 3. 3 (Tenors). 1—Timp. Cym. Trgl. Tbno.—2 Harps—Strings: 16. 16. 12. 12. 12.
Several passages are marked for reduced strings (8. 8. 6. 4. 4) (see note below).

MS: Autograph full score originally with Leuckart (according to contract), now lost. (Untraced by Leuckart or Universal in 1974).

Publication: 1910, F. E. C. Leuckart, Leipzig, full and study scores, 6607, pp. 40.

1921, Transferred to Universal Edition catalogue, full score 6906, study score 6908.

—Re-engraved for miniature score, W. Phil. V. 208, pp. 52, with portrait (1907, full face), introduction and synopsis of form by E(rwin) St(ein).

Performance: 8 September 1909, Hereford, Shire Hall, Three Choirs Festival, LSO, cond. F. Delius.

11 December 1911, Berlin, Blüthnerhalle, Siegmund v. Hausegger.

Arrangements: 'Klavierauszug zu vier Händen von Philip Heseltine', MS DT 45 ff 1–11 (RL 156), pp. 21, n.d. but this version probably 1921 (see Gray 243). Unpublished.
Arranged for 2 pianos (four hands) by Percy Grainger, MS BL Add. 50886, pp. 8, 1922. Published 'Spring 1923', Universal Edition 7142, pp. 23.

The 2-piano arrangement by Percy Grainger marks two cuts as follows: Cue 16 to one bar after cue 17; cue 19 to 6 bars after cue 20. 'Die Stelle zwischen ø und ø kann nach Belieben ausgelassen werden'. Beecham, on the other hand, cut from 2 bars before cue 17 until cue 18.

Notes: PW 129–30 (116–7); TB 166; MC 80. Although the latter incorrectly places the first performance in Hereford Cathedral, the description of the problems arising from the introduction of the Bass Oboe—which also worried Hermann Suter—is a classic. Around this time, too, Beecham had had further difficulties caused by the importing of a sarrusophone (and its player) to our land (MC 71–2, 75–7).
A letter from Hermann Suter to FD, 12 February 1910, '. . . I often find it necessary to use only half the strings and mark down the dynamics . . .' gives the probable origin of the 'small orchestra' passages indicated in the printed score.

A copy of the printed full score marked by Sir Thos. Beecham is in the DT Archive.

VI/19 TWO PIECES FOR SMALL ORCHESTRA
Zwei Stücke für kleines Orchester

[Stimmungsbilder]—(T. & J.'s advertisement on other back covers).

1. On hearing the first Cuckoo in Spring—Beim ersten Kuckucksruf im Frühling (Introducing a Norwegian Folksong)
2. Summer Night on the River—Sommernacht am Flusse

Date: no. 1, 1912; no. 2, 1911 (on printed score). FD to Dr. G. Tischer, 24 June 1913: *One piece is ready, the other not yet . . .*

Dedication: 'For Balfour Gardiner'.

Orchestra: 2 (only 1 in no. 1). 1. 2. 2.—2. 0. 0. 0—Strings.

MS: (*a*). Autograph full score originally with Tischer & Jagenberg, according to the contract, now untraced.

(*b*). Draft score of no. 1 only, Grainger Museum, Melbourne, Australia, n.d. pp. 8, see SM7, 72.

(*c*). A sketch sheet with a rejected harmonization of the folk song for no. 1, DT 39 f 109b (RL 148).

Publication: 1914, Tischer & Jagenburg, Cologne, full score 246/248, pp. 14.

1930, Transferred to Oxford University Press (miniature score also issued).

Performance: 23 October 1913, Leipzig, Gewandhaus, Artur Nikisch (FD to Ernest Newman, 22 October referring to rehearsal, 24 October to the concert).

20 January 1914, London, Philharmonic Society, Willem Mengelberg.

Arrangements: For piano solo, by Gerard Bunk; published 1914, Tischer & Jagenburg 277–8, pp. 11. (Transferred to Oxford University Press in 1930).
For piano duet, by Peter Warlock [Philip Heseltine]; published 1931, Oxford University Press, pp. 15. (MS of no. 2 only, R. Macnutt, Catalogue 104, item 136, pp. 11).

No. 1 only:
For organ, by Eric Fenby; published 1934, Oxford University Press, pp. 7.

For two pianos, by Rudolf Schmidt-Wunstorf; published 1952, Oxford University Press, pp. 8.

For wind band, by Cecil Effinger; published 1969 by Oxford University Press, New York, pp. 14.
Picc. Fl. Ob. Bn.[Bn 2];
Cl 1 (4). Cl 2 (4). Cl 3 (4). BsCl (4). [CB Cl (2)];
2 Hn. Trp 1 (Cornets) (3). Trp. 2 (Cornets) (3). Trb 1 (2). Trb 2 (3). BsTb
String Basses.

For brass band, by Peter Warlock; MS coll. O. W. Neighbour, pp. 10; published 1976 by Oxford University Press, pp. 20.
Soprano Eb cornet; solo, ripieno, 2 & 3 Bb cornets; solo, 1 & 2 Eb horns; 2 Bb baritones; 2 Bb tenor trombones & bass trombone in C; Bb euphonium; Eb & Bb brass basses. (Flugel Horn part by Elgar Howarth added in published score).

147

See: I. A. Copley, 'Warlock and the Brass Band', *Musical Times* (December 1968), 1115–6.

For use of no. 2 in ballet, see *In a Summer Garden*.

Notes: PW 131–2 (118–9); TB 168; SM7, 72.

The Norwegian Folksong used in no. 1 appears in Grieg's setting *I Ola-dalom, i Ola-kjønn*, op. 66 no. 14. The close resemblance between the 'ritornello' of no. 1 and another Grieg piano piece, viz. 'Studenternes Serenade' op. 73 no. 6, has been pointed out by Gerald Abraham (Grieg Symposium, 1948, p. 56 f.n.). FD to Ernest Newman [June 1915]: *you surmise that the Norwegian folk song I have used begins the piece; this is not the case.*

A copy of the printed full scores very fully marked by Sir Thomas Beecham is in the DT Archive.

VI/20 NORTH COUNTRY SKETCHES

1. Autumn (The wind soughs in the trees)
2. Winter Landscape
3. Dance
4. The March of Spring (Woodlands, Meadows and Silent Moors)

Date: nos. 1–2, 1913; nos. 3–4, 1914 (MS).

Dedication: 'Dedicated to Albert Coates'.

Orchestra: nos. 1–2:
2. 2. CA. 2. 2—4. 0. 0. 0—2 Harps (in 2 only)—Strings.
nos. 3–4:
2 (incl. Picc.). 2. CA. 2. 2—4. 2. 3 (Tenors). 1—Timp. Trgl. Tbno (in 3
only). Glockenspiel—2 Harps—Strings.
(Strings: 16. 16. 12. 10. 8, according to MS).

MS: Autograph full score, DT 24 ff 1–46 (RL 87–8), pp. 82, dated *1914
Grez-sur-Loing*.

Publication: 1923, Augener Ltd., London, full score 15927, pp. 76.

1931, ditto, miniature score.

1976, Stainer & Bell, study score (corrected) B457, pp. 76.

Performance: 10 May 1915, London, Queen's Hall, LSO, Thomas
Beecham.

Arrangements: For piano duet, by Philip Heseltine (1921), MS BL Add.
54391, pp. 18 (nos. 1–2), 18, 22. Published 1922 by Augener Ltd., 15660,
pp. 47.

Notes: PW 132–3 (119); TB 168–9.

Corrected proof sheets of the score are to be found in BL H. 403. g; of
the 4-hand piano arrangement in H. 403. (2) and (3) (Philip Heseltine and
Jelka Delius).

A copy of the printed full score marked by Sir Thomas Beecham is in the
DT Archive.

A performance of the work in Frankfurt in 1923 programmed it as
follows:
Nordlandskizzen
(1) Der Herbstwind säuselt in den Bäumen
(2) Winterlandschaft
(3) Tanz
(4) Frühlingseinzug

VI/21 **AIR AND DANCE**
for string orchestra

Date: 1915 (printed score, and copy MS, see below).

Dedication: 'Dedicated to the National Institute for the Blind' (on the printed edition, but not on the earlier MS).

Orchestra: strings only.

MS: (*a*). Draft full score, Grainger Museum, Melbourne, Australia, of an earlier, and somewhat shorter, version than that published, pp. 6.

(*b*). Full score in the hand of Philip Heseltine, DT 25 ff 1–6 (RL 89) pp. 10, dated 1915. With Sir Thomas Beecham's performance markings (some in the hand of Henry Gibson). This copy made in May 1929.

(*c*). *Stichvorlage* in the hand of Eric Fenby, Boosey & Hawkes archive, pp. 6. A pencilled note in Jelka Delius's hand reads: 'Please copy dynamic markings in here from the score belonging to Sir Thomas Beecham.'

Publication: 1931, Boosey & Hawkes (Hawkes Concert Edition), full score 6924, pp. 5 (this incorporates Beecham's markings, see above).

Performance: 1915, London, (privately, at Lady Cunard's), Thomas Beecham.

16 October 1929, London, Aeolian Hall, Sir Thomas Beecham.

Arrangements: For piano solo, by Percy Grainger, MS sold at Sothebys, 16 December 1964, item 398, unpublished.
For piano solo, by Eric Fenby, MS Boosey & Hawkes archive, pp. 6.
Published 1931 by Boosey & Hawkes, 6939, pp. 5.
For flute and piano, or flute and strings, by Eric Fenby, 1976, for James Galway.

Notes: PW 172 (210)—untitled; entry duplicated at (214). SM7, 73.

Date: Spring 1916 (MS).

Dedication: 'For Norman O'Neill'.

Orchestra: 2 (incl. Picc.). 2. CA. 2. 2—4. 2. 3. 1—Timp. BD. Cym. Trgl. SD. Tbno. Glockenspiel—Harp. Celesta—Strings.

MS: Autograph full score, DT 28 ff 1–26 (RL 92), pp. 46, dated *Spring 1916 Grez sur Loing*.

Publication: 1923, Augener Ltd., full score 16045, pp. 33.

1933, ditto, miniature score.

Later impressions of the full score, and the miniature score, include some corrections.

1976, Stainer & Bell, study score (further corrected) B 458, pp. 33.

Performance: 20 October 1923, London, Queen's Hall, Sir Henry J. Wood.

Arrangements: For piano duet, by Philip Heseltine (1921), MS BL Add. 54391, pp. 24. Published 1922 by Augener Ltd., 15824, pp. 20.

Notes: TB 174.

Corrected proof sheets of the score are to be found in BL H. 403. d. (1); of the 4-hand piano arrangement in H. 403. b. (1) and (2) (Philip Heseltine and Jelka Delius).

A copy of the printed full score marked by Sir Thomas Beecham is in the DT Archive.

VI/23 **EVENTYR**
Once upon a time
after Asbjørnsen's Folklore
[A Ballad for Orchestra]—(in MS, not in published score)

Date: 1917 (MS). First sketches 1915, v. Beecham inf.

Dedication: 'For Sir Henry Wood'. (on MS but omitted on early miniature scores; printed on cover of full score).

Orchestra: Picc. 2. 2. CA. 3. BsCl. 3. Sarrusophone—4. 3. 3. 1—Timp. BD. Cym. Trgl. Tamt. SD. Tbno. Xylophone. Glockenspiel. Bells—2 Harps, Celesta—Strings—'20 men's voices (behind) invisible'.

MS: Autograph full score, DT 29 ff 1–27 (RL 93–4), pp. 50, dated *Grez-sur-Loing 1917*.

Publication: 1923, Augener Ltd., full score 16014, pp. 50.

1933, ditto, miniature score (with a few corrections).

1976, Stainer & Bell, study score (extensively corrected) B398, pp. 50.

Performance: 11 January 1919, London, Queen's Hall, Sir Henry J. Wood.

Arrangement: For piano duet, by B. J. Dale; published 1921 by Augener Ltd., 15503, pp. 31.

Notes: TB 172, 181; MC 142; HJW 397–8.

Proof sheets of the score, imperfectly corrected by Jelka Delius, are to be found in BL H. 403. d. (2).

TB 181 states that, having been sketched out 'in a somewhat casual way during . . . 1915, the revised score is on a considerably larger scale than originally planned'.

Source: Asbjørnsen (& Moe): *Norske Folkeeventyr*, 1841 et seq.

A copy of the printed full score marked by Sir Thomas Beecham is in the DT Archive.

For use of this score in a ballet, see under *A Village Romeo & Juliet* above.

VI/24 **A SONG BEFORE SUNRISE**

Date: 1918 (MS).

Dedication: 'For Philip Heseltine'.

Orchestra: 2. 1. 2. 2—2. 0. 0. 0—1 Timp—Strings.

MS: Autograph full score, DT 30 ff 1–6 (RL 95), pp. 12, dated 1918.

Publication: 1922, Augener Ltd., full score 15724, pp. 18.
1932, ditto, miniature score.
Note: at some stage a revised impression of the full score was issued by Augener, correcting most of the errors and attending to inconsistencies of dynamics, etc. The miniature score, so far, remains unrevised.

Performance: 19 September 1923, London, Queen's Hall, Sir Henry J. Wood.

Arrangements: For piano duet, by Philip Heseltine, MS BL Add. 54391, pp. 10. Published 1922 by Augener Ltd., 15723, pp. 11.
For piano solo, by Alan Rowlands; MS arranger, unpublished.
For organ, by Eric Fenby; MS arranger, unpublished.

Notes: TB 182.
Corrected proof sheets of the score are to be found in BL H. 403. a. (3) & (4); of the 4-hand piano arrangement in H. 403. a. (1) & (2). (Philip Heseltine and Jelka Delius).

A copy of the printed full score marked by Sir Thomas Beecham is in the DT Archive.

Date: 1918 (MS). 1918–19 (PW).

> FD to Grainger, 20 July 1918: *I . . . have just finished a new Orchestral work—Poem of Life & Love*. Jelka Delius to Marie Clews, 30 July 1918: 'Fred has quite finished his Symphony. He calls it "A poem of Life and Love". . .'

Dedication: none.

Orchestra: 3. 2. CA. 3. BsCl. 3. Sarrusophone—4. 3. 3 (Tenors). 1—Timp. BD—2 Harps—Strings.

MS: (*a*). Autograph full score, dated 1918, pp. 50, now defective; pp. 1–27 and 48–50 in DT 31 ff 1–23 (RL 96–98), with many deletions and alterations; pp. 44–47 now Bodleian Library, Dept. of Western Manuscripts, MS Don. b. 2; pp. 28–43 missing.

> (*b*). Copy in the hand of Jelka Delius, pp. 1–20, of portion corresponding approximately to pp. 1–27 of the autograph, DT 31 ff 24–33 (RL ibid.).

> (*c*). 4 pages of sketches *(Slow movement-symphonie)*, DT 39 ff 87–8 (RL 146).

Publication: none. Facsimile of first page of original score, RL 96.

Performance: none. It is interesting to note, however, that the score has blue-pencil rehearsal numbers.

Arrangement: For two pianos, four hands, by Balfour Gardiner, 1928. 2 copies, unfinished, completed by Eric Fenby, DT 32 ff 1–25 (RL 100). The first 13 pages of this arrangement agree in essence with the 20 pages of Jelka Delius's score (*b*) above; this arrangement is thus apparently the only surviving complete version of the *Poem of Life and Love* as originally conceived. Unpublished. For this arrangement, see EF 17, 27 and *plates 21 and 22*.

Notes: PW 174 (212) states 'MS (lost)'.
TB 182; EF 17, 29, 34, 44, 49–50.

Material from this work was used for *A Song of Summer*, 1929–30, q.v.

VI/26 **A SONG OF SUMMER**

Date: 1929 (MS); 1930 (printed score).

Dedication: none.

Orchestra: 3 (incl. picc). 2. CA. 3. BsCl. 3. Contra—4. 3. 3. 1—Timp.—
Harp—Strings.

MS: (*a*). Short score of first work based on part of *Poem of Life and Love*,
MS in the hand of Eric Fenby, DT 32 ff 26–30 (RL 101).

(*b*). Full score, first version (and sketches) entitled *A Song of Summer*,
in the hand of Eric Fenby, DT 31 ff 34–43 (RL 99), pp. 18; but now
lacking pp. 12–17 inclusive (pp. 12–15 = pp. 44–7 of *Poem of Life and
Love*, v. supra, now in the Bodleian Library, and pp. 16–17 = pp. 48–9
ibid., now restored to that work).

(*c*). Full score, final version, in the hand of Eric Fenby, DT 33 ff 1–26/27
(RL 102–3) pp. 17, dated 1929.

(*d*). *Stichvorlage* in the hand of Eric Fenby, Boosey & Hawkes archives,
pp. 20.

Publication: 1931, Boosey & Hawkes, full score 6931, pp. 20.
ca. 1943, ditto, issued as miniature score 8830, HPS 53.

Performance: 17 September 1931, London, Queen's Hall, BBC Orchestra,
Sir Henry J. Wood.

Arrangement: For two pianos, four hands, by Eric Fenby, 1929; 2 copies,
DT 32 ff 31–47/48 (RL 101). Unpublished.

Notes: TB 207; HJW 399; EF 44–5, 49–50, 82, 111, 132–47, 206.

The published and final version of the opening was a later dictation, see
EF 82, 132–47. Full score of this section was also printed in miniature in
appendix to EF [236]. Facsimile of first page of MS score, RL 102.

Plate 21: Poem of Life and Love, arrangement for two pianos. The last page of the portion arranged by Balfour Gardiner

156

Plate 22: Poem of Life and Love, arrangement for two pianos. The first page of Eric Fenby's contribution

157

VI/27 **IRMELIN**
Prelude
(originally 'Intermezzo from *Irmelin*', according to contract).

Date: Autumn 1931 (EF 112).

Dedication: none.

Orchestra: 2. 1. CA. 2. BsCl. 2.—2. 0. 0. 0—Harp—Strings.
(CA and BsCl are cued in; parts for optional Trp. and Trb. to replace Horns).

MS: (*a*). Full score in the hand of Eric Fenby, Boosey & Hawkes archives, pp. 8 oblong; also piano conductor, pp. 3.

(*b*). *Stichvorlage* in the hand of Harold Perry, Boosey & Hawkes archives, pp. 11.

Publication: 1938, Boosey & Hawkes (Hawkes Concert Edition), full score 8000, pp. 11.

1946, ditto, miniature score 9065 issued in HPS 86 ('Three Orchestral Pieces') pp. 34–43.

Performance: 23 September 1935, London, Royal Opera House; as an interlude in Act III of *Koanga* (q.v.), Beecham.

1 April 1937, London, Queen's Hall, LPO, Beecham (substituting second movement of *Florida*.)

Arrangements: For piano solo, by Eric Fenby, MS Boosey & Hawkes archives, pp. 4. Published 1938 by Boosey & Hawkes, 14791, pp. 5.
For organ, by Eric Fenby, MS Boosey & Hawkes archives, pp. 4. Published 1938 by Boosey & Hawkes, 8063, pp. 5.

Notes: TB 208; EF 112.

This work is based on four themes from the opera *Irmelin*, using parts of the preludes to Acts 1 & 3 thereof.

For use of this score in a ballet, see under *A Village Romeo & Juliet* above.

VI/28 FANTASTIC DANCE

Date: 1931 (printed copy); late 1931 (EF 112).

Dedication: 'To Eric Fenby'.

Orchestra: 2. 2. 2. 2—4. 2. 3. 1—Timp. BD. Cym. Glockenspiel—Harp—Strings.

MS: Full score in the hand of Eric Fenby, Boosey & Hawkes archives, pp. 17; also piano conductor, pp. 8.

Publication: 1933, Boosey & Hawkes (Hawkes Concert Edition) 7268, parts and piano conductor (pp. 6) only; full score unpublished.

Performance: 12 January 1934, London, BBC Symphony Orchestra, Adrian C. Boult.

Arrangement: For two pianos four hands by Ethel Bartlett and Rae Robertson. Published 1936 by Boosey & Hawkes, 14517, pp. 8.

Notes: TB 208; EF 112, 215.

According to Herbert Hughes' article 'New Compositions by Delius' in the *Daily Telegraph*, 23 January 1932, p. 13, this work was 'sketched a few years ago and only completed (with Mr. Fenby's assistance) within the last twelve months'. The opening bars (with the unusual—for FD—use of the whole-tone scale progressions) existed in a sketch in Delius's hand, as did the germ of the middle section (verbal information from Eric Fenby to the writer).

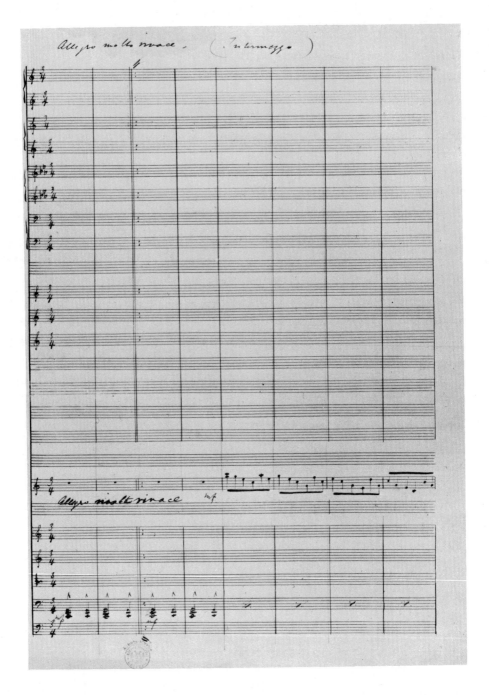

Plate 23: Suite for Violin and Orchestra. First page of the second movement

160

VII Works for solo instrument(s) and orchestra:

VII/1 [SUITE]
[for Violin and Orchestra]

1. Pastorale   Andante quasi allegretto   (E minor)
2. Intermezzo   Allegro molto vivace   (C major)
3. [Elegie]   Adagio cantabile   (G major)
4. [Finale]   Allegro animato   (G major)

Date: 1888 (PW).

Dedication: ?none.

Orchestra: 3. 2. 2. 2—4. 2. 3. 1—Timp.—Solo violin—Strings.

MS: Autograph full score, DT 3 ff 1–46 (RL 22–24) pp. 89, lacking titlepage; [n.d.]. Also separate violin part, ibid., ff 47–50.

Publication: none. Facsimile of first page of MS score, RL 22. See also plate 23.

Performance: none as far as known; although the existence of the separate violin part, with bowings and some alterations, points to the possibility of at least a "read through".

Notes: PW 160 (198) ("Pastorale"); TB 173.

The second movement is a later insertion. The solo figuration in this movement slightly resembles that used in the closing section of the Violin Concerto of 1916; also of *A Mass of Life*, Violins 1 before cue no. 25 (full score p. 44). Still closer is the similarity to the Cello Concerto, bars 128 sqq., even to the subsequent "taking over" by the woodwind of the soloist's figure. *See plate 23.*

VII/2 **LÉGENDES (SAGEN)**
pour piano & orchestre.

(F sharp major)

Date: 1890 (MS).

Dedication: none.

Orchestra: 3 (incl. Picc). 2. 2. 2—4. 2. 3. 1—Timp. Cym. Trgl. Tambour—
Piano (solo)—Strings.

MS: Autograph pencil draft score, DT 39 ff 24–49 (RL 138–9), pp. 1–51,
dated. Incomplete: (two 24-page sections followed by two loose leaves).

Publication: }
Performance: } none.

Notes: PW 160 (198); TB 59.

The elaborate piano part, basically a series of extensive variations on the
opening theme in F sharp major, is almost complete as far as the work
goes; the orchestral accompaniment is often fragmentary. A middle
section, in E flat major, appears to be on the point of re-introducing the
opening theme when the MS ceases.
A chromatic phrase from one of the variations is used in *The Magic
Fountain* as Talum Hadjo utters his words of warning in Act II thereof.
See plates 2 and 3 where the relevant phrases are placed side by side.

VII/3 **LÉGENDE**
[in E flat]—(printed copy only)
pour Violon & Orchestre

Date: 1892 (Chop); 1893 (PW); 1895 (MS score).

Dedication: none.

Orchestra: 2. 2. 2. 2—4. 0. 0. 0—Timp.—Solo violin—Strings.
In the autograph MS, the clarinet staves appear throughout *above* those of the "hautboys".

MS: Autograph full score, DT 8 ff 18 (RL 41–2) pp. 34, dated *Paris 1895*.
Signature (later) altered to *Frederick Delius*.

Publication: 1916, Forsyth Bros. Ltd., for violin and pianoforte, pp. 9, 4.
Orchestral score unpublished.
Facsimile of first page of MS, RL 42.

Performance: 30 May 1899, London, St. James's Hall, John Dunn, cond. Alfred Hertz.
Note: an earlier performance referred to in correspondence, e.g. FD to Jutta Bell [Dec. 1896] writes: *Johannes Wolff is playing my "Legende" for Orchestra & Violin in London in January*; also W. Augener to FD, 19 November 1896: 'I will endeavour to hear your Légende in January.'

Notes: PW 134–5 (120); TB 62–3; Chop 18, item 1.

By his reference together with the Violin Sonata in B and *Paa Vidderne*, both finished in 1892, Beecham implies this also to be the date of the *Légende*. Was it first written for Violin and Piano, and only scored for orchestral accompaniment in 1895?

VII/4 PIANO CONCERTO KLAVIERKONZERT
in C minor C moll

Date: 1897 on early MSS and published editions, though revised before 1904 and again 1906–7 and 1909.

Dedication: 'Theodor Szántó gewidmet' (on published editions).

Orchestra: *Original version* (first score):
3. 2. 2. BsCl. 3–4. 2. 3 (Tenors). 1—Timp—Strings—Piano solo.
Published version (first edition):
3. 2. 2. 3—4. 2. 3. 1—Timp. Cym.—Piano solo—Strings. The later published editions added CA. and BD.
Note: in view of the complex history of this work, arrangements are not shown separately in this case.

MS: (*A*). Autograph full score of **Fantasy for Orchestra & piano forte,** probably earliest version, DT 11 ff 1–38 (RL 55–6) pp. 75, dated *Fritz Delius 1897*. This version is in one movement of several sections; the basic thematic material being as now familiar from the later publications, though the layout always, and the key-relations often, differ.

(*a*). Separate piano part of the above, principally in the hand of the 'Paris copyist', DT 10 ff 20–37 (RL 51, 53), pp. 23, dated *Fritz Delius 1897*. Delius himself added, on separate sheets, rewritten versions of the slow central portion (facsimile of a page in DLP 38) and the final cadenza. *See plate 24.*

The earliest public performances of the work were of a version recast into 3 separate movements, viz.
(i) Allegro ma non troppo (C minor)
(ii) Largo (D flat major)
(iii) Maestoso con moto (5/4)(C minor)
(The material of this third movement was largely new).

(*B*). Full score of this 3 movement version untraced at present and presumed lost.

(*bb*). *Arrangement* for two pianos four hands of (*B*) above, by Julius Buths, DT 10 ff 1–19 (RL 50–51, 53) pp. 36, dated *Spring 1897*. Although in three separate movements the musical content of movements (i) and (ii) agrees fairly closely with the corresponding portions of the later publications.
(This third movement is, unfortunately, now defective; only 5 pages surviving.)

Before publication in 1907, further rewriting took place. Delius returned to the one-movement form, and the solo part was rewritten by Theodor Szántó (FD to Percy Grainger, 29 April 1914: *Szanto arranged the Klaviersatz most beautifully and made it much more effective*).

(*C*). The *Stichvorlage* for the first publication, however, originally with Verlag Harmonie according to the contract, is now lost. (So is the MS of a later version prepared by Szántó but rejected by Delius).

(*D*). Copy in an unidentified copyist's hand of the revised score of the published version, Grainger Museum, Melbourne, Australia, dated *Wien 1914*. Photocopy of this MS, DT 41, pp. 82 (RL 152).

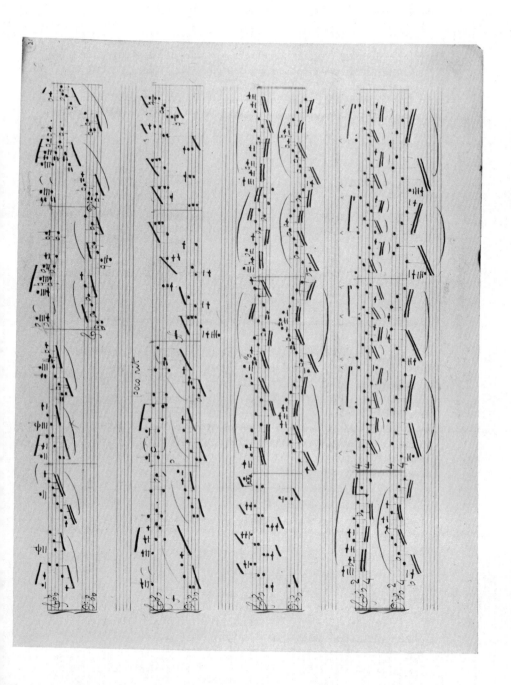

Plate 24: Piano Concerto (1897). Second page of separate solo part in the hand of the 'Paris copyist'

165

Publication: *Original versions* unpublished.

Facsimile of a page from final cadenza of *Fantasy* (MS *A* above), RL 56. This reveals the passage subsequently used in the Violin Concerto of 1916, after cue no. 20. (cf. PW 137 (122)).

Facsimiles of the first and last extant pages from the rejected Third movement, in the arrangement for two pianos four hands (MS *bb* above), RL 50, 52.

See also under MS (*a*) above (DLP 38 and plate 24).

Revised version:

1907, Verlag Harmonie, Berlin, full score (no no.) (lithographed) pp. 61, dated 1897.

1907, ditto, Klavierauszug für 2 Klaviere zu 4 Händen von Otto Singer, 'Klaviersatz bearbeitet von Theodor Szántó', 180 (Stich u. Druck von C. G. Röder), pp. 38, dated 1897.

Various post-performance alterations were made, though not all that Szántó first wanted; and fresh impressions of the piano part were apparently printed (ca. 1909) though not a definitive full score at this stage.

FD to Jelka Delius, Oct. 1913 . . . *he* [Hertzka] *engraves the piano concerto quite new.*

1921, Transferred to Universal Edition catalogue; full score (updated by having the alterations pasted over or interlined) 3901; two piano arrangement with Ger. and Eng. directions (instead of Ger. only), corrections etc. (reprinted by Breitkopf and Härtel) 3903, pp. 38, dated 1897.

Note: not all UE prints of the 2-piano score acknowledge Szántó's contribution. The note relating was first put on the titlepage; then, when the titlepage layout was changed, these words were omitted; being later restored to the head of the first page.

1951, Full score engraved for 'Complete Works. Revised and Edited by Sir Thomas Beecham, Bart.', Boosey & Hawkes, London, 8864, pp. 68.

1975, Miniature score, reduced from above, with some further corrections, HPS 895.

1975, Reduction for two pianos by Otto Singer. Solo part arranged by Theodor Szántó. Re-engraved to incorporate Sir Thomas Beecham's revision and editing, Boosey & Hawkes, 20214, pp. 43.

Performance: (version in 3 movements).

24 October 1904, Elberfeld, Stadthalle, Julius Buths, Elberfelder Konzertgesellschaft, cond. Hans Haym

(published version).

22 October 1907, London, Queen's Hall Orchestra, Theodor Szántó, cond. Henry J. Wood.

Notes: PW 37 (54), 137 (122), 164 (202); TB 97, 99, 125, 132, 135–6, 145; EF 57–8.

Chop 19, item 3: 'Das Werk ist im Winter 1906/7 vom Komponisten mit Verwerfung der ersten Faktur vollständig umgearbeitet worden'.

That the 3-movement version was still intact in early 1906 is seen from a letter to FD from Marie Geselschap, 2 April 1906, asking 'whether you want the Third Movement . . . very slow, and whether you want to leave the *Cadenza* at the end as it is and have it played quasi impromptu?' For more detailed consideration of the many differences—some small, some large—between the various MSS, versions and publications, see: Robert Threlfall, 'Delius's second thoughts, and an unknown version of his piano concerto,' *Musical Opinion*, 93, 1115 (August 1970), pp. 579, 581; and 'Delius's piano concerto: a postscript,' *ibid*, 95, 1129 (October 1971) pp. 14–15; reprinted (condensed and revised) in *A Delius Companion*, pp. 239–247.

VII/5 CONCERTO FOR VIOLIN, VIOLONCELLO AND ORCHESTRA
(Double Concerto for Violin & Violoncello)

Date: 1915 (MS); 1915–16 (PW).

Dedication: 'For May & Beatrice Harrison.' (Omitted, presumably in error, from miniature score, it appears on MS and piano score).

Orchestra: 2. 1. CA. 2. 2—4. 2. 3. 1—Timp.—Harp—Solo Vl. Solo Vc.—Strings.

MS: Autograph full score, DT 26 ff 1–39 (RL 90) pp. 73, dated 1915. Frequent amendments to both solo parts. Facsimile of an excerpt, DLP 70.

Publication: 1922, Augener Ltd., London, full score 15741, pp. 55.

1932, ditto, miniature score ditto.
Numerous small errors disfigure these first editions.

1976, Stainer & Bell, study score (corrected) B399, pp. 55.

Performance: 21 February 1920, London, Queen's Hall, May and Beatrice Harrison, cond. Sir Henry Wood.

Arrangements: For violin, cello and piano by Philip Heseltine (1915), MS BL Add. 54391, pp. 30. Published 1920 by Augener Ltd., 15340, pp. 29, 7, 8. Cello solo part arranged by Lionel Tertis for viola, published 1935 by Augener Ltd, 17496, pp. 8; same piano score with reworded cover and titlepage ('violin, viola and pianoforte').

Notes: PW 137–9 (122–3); TB 174.

A copy of the printed full score marked by Sir Thomas Beecham is in the DT Archive.

Proof sheets of the parts, corrected by Jelka Delius, are to be found in BL H. 403. b. (3).

VII/6 VIOLIN CONCERTO

Date: 1916 (MS).

Dedication: 'For Albert Sammons'.

Orchestra: 2. 1. CA. 2. 2—4. 2. 3. 1—Timp.—Harp—Solo Vl.—Strings (12. 12. 10. 8. 6 according to Heseltine's edition).

MS: Autograph full score, DT 27 ff 1–29 (RL 91) pp. 49, dated 1916. Some amendments to the solo part.

Publication: 1921, Augener Ltd., London, full score 15569, pp. 45.

1932, ditto, miniature score ditto.
Numerous small errors disfigure these first editions.

1975, Stainer & Bell, study score (corrected). B 355, pp. 45.

Performance: 30 January 1919, London, Queen's Hall, Royal Philharmonic Society, Albert Sammons, cond. Adrian C. Boult.

Arrangement: For violin and piano by Philip Heseltine (1919), MS BL Add. 54391, pp. 26. Published 1919 by Augener Ltd., 15239, pp. 24, 8. Some slight alterations made in reprints, and more numerous corrections taken up in the 1976 reissue (Stainer & Bell no. 1940).

Notes: PW 139–40 (123–4); TB 173–4.

Proof sheets corrected by Delius are to be found in BL H. 403. e. (2) (for the score) and H. 403 (1) (for the violin and piano arrangement).
Beecham suggested a cut from one bar before cue 38 to cue 40, in a printed score marked by him and now in the DT archive.
Later impressions of the violin and piano version incorporate some altered readings, probably for expediency, in the solo part, e.g. the double stop at cue 3; the bar before cue 10; the bar at 3 before cue 11. Likewise, the horn note originally at cue 20 in this version was deleted in the MS full score; it was a 'left-over' from an earlier version of the preceding bars (now pasted over), to which it formed the end of the horn line.

VII/7 CELLO CONCERTO

Date: 1921 (MS copy).
Sketched Grez, March 1920 'at the request of Beatrice Harrison' (TB 188); composed Spring 1921 in London, see Jelka Delius to N. O'Neill, 30 March 1923.

Dedication: none.

Orchestra: 2. 1. CA. 2. 2—4. 2. 3. 1—Timp.—Harp—Solo Vc.—Strings.

MS: (*a*). Autograph full score, signed and dated, included on 1952 list; also sketches. ?Beecham library.

(*b*). *Stichvorlage* in the hand of C. W. Orr, with pencilled additions of phrasing marks (? by FD, v. inf.), Universal Edition Archiv, on loan to the British Library, Loan 54/5, pp. 78, dated 1921.
Note: 'Delius asked me to make a fair copy of his score from his MS in the summer of 1921, when I was staying at a hotel not far from him in Hampstead . . . In my hurry to get the thing done I inadvertently left out masses of the phrasing marks . . .' (C. W. Orr to present writer, 'March 24th' [1970]).

Publication: 1922, Universal Edition, Vienna, full score 7023, pp. 59.

Performance: 31 January 1923, Vienna, Alexandre Barjansky, cond. Ferdinand Löwe. FD to P. Heseltine, 26 February 1923. . . [Barjansky] *played* [the Cello Concerto] *with great success in Vienna on January 31st.*

1 March 1923, Frankfurt, Alexandre Barjansky, cond. Paul Klenau.

3 July 1923, London, Beatrice Harrison, cond. Eugène Goossens.

Arrangements: For cello and piano by Philip Heseltine, 1923. MS listed on second list of 1935; published 1923 by Universal Edition, 7021, pp. 22, 6.

1935, Reissued, with a new edition of the solo part by Herbert Withers, 7021a, pp. 6.

1952, Transferred to Boosey & Hawkes. Cello and piano edition, with original and new versions of the solo part, issued as 18399/a/b.
Note: the Withers version, though posthumously published, had Delius's 'imprimatur', according to Eric Fenby, and dates from 1932.

Notes: PW 140 (124); TB 188–9.
Note the similarity of figuration at bars 128 ff, with the second movement of the Suite for violin and orchestra (v. supra p. 161).
Delius told Eric Fenby that the 16-bar introduction was an 'afterthought'. Referring to the '60th birthday' concert in Frankfurt, Jelka Delius wrote to Adine O'Neill on 2 July 1922: 'The Violoncello concerto will also be ready by then' [i.e. by 29 January 1923]. FD (JD) to Norman O'Neill [n.d. but spring 1923]: *Barjansky brought it out in Vienna & played it in Frankfurt.* Ibid., v. Derek Hudson, *Norman O'Neill,* p. 71, 20 August 1922: *Would the Philharmonic like to give the first performance of my Cello Concerto with Beatrice Harrison? Perhaps in March? Universal Edition is publishing it & I have just corrected the proofs.*

VII/8 CAPRICE and ELEGY
Two pieces for violoncello solo and chamber orchestra.

Date: 1930 (printed score).

Dedication: 'Dedicated to Beatrice Harrison'.

Orchestra: 1. 1. CA. 1. 1—2. 0. 0. 0—Harp—Solo cello—Strings (6 Vl. 2 Va. 2 Vc. 1 CB).

MS: Full score in the hand of Eric Fenby, Boosey & Hawkes archives, pp. 10.

Publication: 1931, Boosey & Hawkes (Hawkes Concert Edition), full score, 6930, pp. 19.
[1943] ditto, miniature score issued, 8829, as HPS 54.

Performance: played on tour in USA in 1930 by Beatrice Harrison.
23 April 1931, London, Wigmore Hall, Beatrice Harrison (with piano).

Arrangements: For cello and piano by Eric Fenby, MSS (2 separate items) Boosey & Hawkes archives. Published 1931 by Boosey & Hawkes, 'solo part edited by Herbert Withers', 6932–3, pp. 3, 1; 4, 1.

For viola and piano by Lionel Tertis, published 1934 by Boosey & Hawkes (a different engraving of the piano score). 7558–9, pp. 3, 1; 4, 1.

Elegy only, arranged for 5 cellos by Eric Fenby as a memorial to Douglas Cameron, 1974, MS arranger.

Notes: TB 208; EF 102.

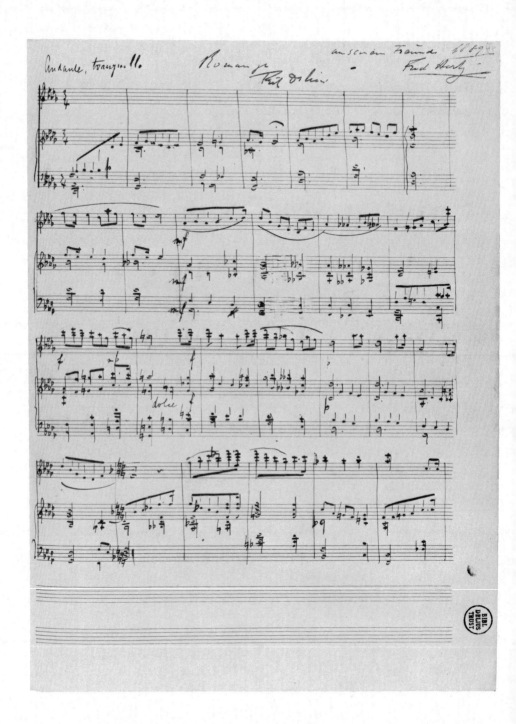

Plate 25 : Romance for violin and piano. First page of score

VIII Chamber music:

VIII/1 [STRING QUARTET]
1. [lost]
2. Allegro Vivace   (?G minor)
3. Adagio con molto espressione (C minor)
4. Agitato Allegro   (C minor)

Date: 1888. FD to Grieg (n.d. but 1888): *I have a string quartet ready.* Grieg to FD, 30 Dec. 1888: 'And you have written a string quartet.'

Dedication: ?none.

MS: Autograph DT 35 ff 1–6 (RL 110–1), orig. pp. 29, now defective. Wanting first movement, and second movement except last 11 bars of middle section, with da capo indicated. Some pencilled alterations in another hand (?Sinding's, v. inf.).

Publication: none. Facsimile of last page of (2) in DLP 20.

Performance: none as far as known.

Notes: TB 49; not in PW. Sinding wrote to FD on 28 December 1888 '... some stoppings are impossible to execute'; returning the score to Delius on 15 April 1889, Sinding wrote: 'In a few places I have, as you wanted me to, altered the parts'.

The fragment still surviving of the middle section of the second movement shows that this was used in 1916 as the basis of the principal theme for the second movement of another (published) string quartet, v. inf.

VIII/2 ROMANCE
pour Violon [and pianoforte]

Andante, tranquillo—   (D flat—F major)
più vivo—   (A minor)
Andante molto tranquillo & dolce (C major)

Date: 1889 (MS).

Dedication: 'an seinem Freunde Fred Hertz'.

MS: Autograph DT 35 ff 7–10 (RL 111) pp. 5 dated 1889.

Publication: none as far as known. Facsimile of first page, *plate 25*.

Performance: none as far as known.

Notes: PW 164 (202), giving the date incorrectly as 1896.

VIII/3 **SONATA**
in H dur [in B major]

Violin and pianoforte

1. Allegro con brio   (B major)
2. Andante molto tranquillo (F sharp major)
3. Allegro con moto   (B major)

Date: 1892 (MS).

Dedication: ?none.

MS: (*a*). Autograph, Beecham libr. list 'Sonata in H dur, 1892'. Eric Fenby recalls the MS, neatly written on oblong paper, was bound in dark brown hard covers.

(*b*). Copy in the hand of William Borner, made in 1957, coll. Wilfred Lehmann, pp. 47; microfilm DT.

(*c*). The MS of a violin sonata (unspecified, but probably this work) was formerly in the collection of the late Mrs. Harold Bauer, but is untraced since her death.

Publication: Offered to C. F. Peters, Leipzig, but declined (Dr. Max Abraham to FD, 28 February 1893).

1977, Boosey & Hawkes 20356, pp. 44, 16. The violin part edited by David C. Stone.

Performance: Privately, in Harold Bauer's rooms, Paris 1893.
Broadcast, 1957 and 12 April 1958, BBC London, Wilfred and Bernice Lehmann.

21 March 1975, London, Holborn Library, Delius Society, David C. Stone and Robert Threlfall.

Notes: PW 29, 162 (48, 200); TB 62–3.
'Grieg . . . was really annoyed about Dr. Abraham and your Sonata' (Nina Grieg to FD, 8 April 1893). [In 1891, Dr. Abraham had rejected FD's songs, as hundreds were published in Germany each year, recommending chamber or piano music as wiser to start with. According to Sinding's letter to FD of 16 April 1893, it was Grieg's wish that the Sonata should be published, and 'he was actually furious with Dr. Abraham' that his words were misconstrued and the work 'despite its undoubted talent and beauty' was declined as 'not good publishable material', according to Dr. Abraham].

In the *meno mosso* of the first movement occurs a reference to *Irmelin*, Act III, 596; the opening of the last movement recalls the orchestral *Paa Vidderne*.

VIII/4 [STRING QUARTET]

Date: 1892–3.

Notes: Heseltine mentions and lists a quartet of this period (PW 29 (48); 162 (200), dated 1893, as '(No. 1)'), but not an earlier one. Beecham refers to the published quartet of 1916–17 as 'the third of its kind so far as we know' (TB 173); but beside the quartet of 1888 (to which he refers, TB 49) and another quartet implied as being written in 1892 (TB 62) he has a reference (TB 52) to work on a new quartet at a period implied as 1889. Eric Fenby, in a sleeve-note to a recording of the published quartet, speaks of 'three other' quartets!
Some pages of pencil drafts, now bound into DT 39 at ff 60, 85–6 (RL 142, 146) are marked by Fenby 'Rejected sketches string quartet', but they resemble in style and rhythm the second movement of the published quartet (which movement was certainly added to that work later, q.v.).

VIII/5 ROMANCE
Cello and pianoforte

Lento tranquillo—	(B major)
Molto tranquillo—	(E major)
Tempo I°	(B major)

Date: 1896 (MS).

Dedication: 'Dediée à Monsieur Joseph Hollman.'

MS: Autograph DT 35 ff 11–14 (RL 111) pp. 7, dated 1896.
The MS has clearly been annotated by an engraver showing divisions into systems and pages, as if in preparation for publication.

Publication: 1976, Boosey & Hawkes 20336, pp. 6, 3.

Performance: 22 June 1976, Helsinki Festival; Julian Lloyd Webber, Timo Mikkila; repeated 24 June, London, Purcell Room; Julian Lloyd Webber, Yitkin Seow.

Notes: PW 164 (202); EF 68.

VIII/6 SONATA
[no. 1]
Violin and pianoforte
1. With easy movement but not quick—
2. Slow
3. With vigour and animation

Date: 1914 (printed copy). Also see below.

Dedication: none.

MS: (*a*). Autograph pencil sketches, DT 34 ff 1–12 (RL 107), undated but attributed to 1905, for most of movements 1 and 2 only.

(*b*). Copy in the hand of Philip Heseltine, DT 34 ff 13–35 (RL 107), pp. 45, dated 1915, complete.

Publication: 1917, Forsyth Bros. [no number], pp. 21, 7. 'The pianoforte part edited and revised by R. J. Forbes. The violin part revised and fingered by Arthur Catterall.'

Performance: 1915, Manchester, A. Catterall and R. J. Forbes.

Notes: PW 136 (121); TB 174.
Uncorrected proof sheets are bound into DT 34, ff 51–77; a printed copy marked by Sir Thomas Beecham is also in the DT Archive.
May Harrison (RCM Magazine, 1937, no. 2; reprinted in *A Delius Companion*), referring to her first performance (with Hamilton Harty) of the work in London, mentions that Harty 'spent hours editing and correcting the piano part (MS) . . . Delius carried it off . . . to send it direct to the publishers; but by some extraordinary chance, the wrong part got published, and, as far as I know, Harty's wonderful work was irretrievably lost'.

VIII/7 SONATA
Violoncello and pianoforte
Allegro, ma non troppo— (D major)
Lento, molto tranquillo—
Tempo I

Date: 1916 (printed copy) (doubtless following MS). PW, TB both 1917.

Dedication: 'For Beatrice Harrison'.

MS: Untraced; presumably formerly Winthrop Rogers archives. One leaf, autograph, (recto, p. 3, basically as bars 35–52 of the published work, but verso, p. 4, different and rejected material) now bound into DT 39 f 68 (RL 143). Some sketches, including notes for 'last movement' (not used), are now in the Grainger Museum (see SM7, 74).

Publication: 1919, Winthrop Rogers, London, 4020, pp. 15, 7.
[?1919], Universal Edition, Vienna, 6923 (this is an entirely different engraving from the Winthrop Rogers edition).
Note: after Boosey & Hawkes absorbed Winthrop Rogers, the former reprinted the work unaltered until the 1973 issue, which corrected most of the errors in the original plates. (The sharp to the C in the first L.H chord, and similarly on p. 11, is marked in a copy formerly belonging to Evlyn Howard-Jones with the annotation: '♯ (F.D.)'. The last chord in the cello part, traditionally omitted, is deleted in the same hand in this copy).

Performance: November 1918, London, Wigmore Hall, Beatrice Harrison and Evlyn Howard-Jones.
8 June 1920, Paris, Beatrice Harrison.

Notes: TB 181.
A printed copy marked by Sir Thomas Beecham is in the DT Archive.

See Supplementary Catalogue

31 Oct 1918, Harrison, Harty, Wigmore Hall

VIII/8 **STRING QUARTET**

1. With animation
2. Quick and lightly
3. LATE SWALLOWS. Slow and wistfully
4. Very quick and vigorously

Date: 1916 (MS and printed score); 1916–17 (PW).

Dedication: none.

MS: (*a*). Autograph score, original version, dated 'Grez-sur-Loing 1916', with DT in 1944 (v. *Tempo* no. 7, June 1944, p. 25); included on Beecham Libr. list. This MS differs 'in innumerable instances—melodic, harmonic and textural—from the' published score. The second movement of the latter 'does not occur in this MS; on the other hand it contains two versions of the slow movement, "Late Swallows", one considerably shorter than the other'. (*Tempo*, loc. cit.)

(*b*). *Stichvorlage* of the revised version, possibly at least in part in a copyist's hand, formerly with Augeners for engraving, but apparently lost by 1964; as it was not included in the transfer of MSS from them to the DT Archive which took place that year.

Note: as the tempo direction of 'Late Swallows' given in the review of the first performance (*Musical Times*, Dec. 1916, p. 554) was 'with slow, waving movement'—now the direction of the middle section—it appears that this movement may have originally lacked the opening pages. An autograph MS short score draft of these pages only, to be found in a sketchbook in the Grainger Museum (v. appendix inf. and SM7, 75), may support this view.

Examples of the textural differences abovementioned can be seen in the following:

(α). A page of pencil autograph draft score representing part of pp. 40–1 of the published work, now bound into DT 39 as f 84 a (RL 145);

(β). Four similar pencil autograph draft score pages representing the last six pages of the first movement as printed, now also in the Grainger Museum, see SM7, 73;

(γ). A page of the original fair copy autograph score reproduced in facsimile in *Tempo* (loc. cit.), representing part of pages 26–7 of the printed score. *See plate 26.*

FD to P. Heseltine 27 May 1917 . . . *I have rewritten my string quartet and added a scherzo—I heard it in Paris—there was a little too much double-stopping—I think it is now good.*

Publication: 1922, Augener Ltd., miniature score 16074, pp. 41, and parts 15746, pp. 12, 12, 12, 12. Reprinted (unaltered) by Galliard (Stainer & Bell).

Performance: *Original version in 3 movements:*
17 November 1916, London, Aeolian Hall, London String Quartet (Albert Sammons, H. Wynn Reeves, Waldo Warner, C. Warwick Evans).

Revised version in 4 movements:
1 February 1919, London, Aeolian Hall, London String Quartet.

Plate 26: String Quartet. A page from the original score of the movement 'Late Swallows'

Arrangement: 'Late Swallows' arranged for string orchestra by Eric Fenby, published 1963 by Galliard Ltd., score 18769, pp. 11. A similar arrangement of the remaining 3 movements is currently (1977) available on hire from the publishers (Stainer & Bell).

Notes: TB 173–4; 181. SM7, 73. *Tempo*, loc. cit.
Philip Heseltine to FD, 15 May 1918 '. . . since the *String Quartet* was raped by that lecherous party of players in London . . .'
The opening theme of the second movement is based on part of an earlier quartet of 1888, q.v.
For evolution of the central melody of the third movement, see: Robert Threlfall, 'Late Swallows in Florida', *Composer* 51, Spring 1974, pp. 25–7, where links stretching as far back as the *Florida* Suite and *The Magic Fountain*, likewise *Koanga*, are examined. I am indebted to Mr. A. G. Lovgreen, also, who has pointed out the resemblance of some of this material to the opening of 'Marching through Georgia'.
Proofs corrected by Jelka Delius are to be found in the British Library, H. 403. x. (1) (score) and H. 403. e. (1) (parts).

VIII/9 **SONATA no. 2**
Violin and pianoforte

Con moto— (C major)
Lento—
Molto vivace

Date: 1923 (MS).

Dedication: none.

MS: In the hand of Jelka Delius, Boosey & Hawkes archives, pp. 18, dated.

Publication: 1924, Hawkes & Sons 6260, pp. 12, 4. 'Edited by Albert Sammons and Evlyn Howard-Jones.' The 1973 reprint corrected the few errors in the original plates.

Performance: 7 October 1924, Westminster Music Society. Albert Sammons and Evlyn Howard-Jones.

Arrangement: 'Adapted and edited for Viola' and piano by Lionel Tertis, published 1932 by Boosey & Hawkes 7207, pp. 12, 7. (Separate viola part issued with original piano score).

Note: TB 193; A printed copy marked by Sir Thomas Beecham is in the DT Archive.

VIII/10 **SONATA no. 3**
Violin and pianoforte

1. Slow
2. Andante scherzando—Meno mosso
3. Lento—Con moto

Date: 1930 (March—EF).

Dedication: 'For May Harrison.'

MS: (*a*). In the hand of Eric Fenby, DT 34 ff 78–88 (RL 109) pp. 20, dated.

(*b*). *Stichvorlage* in the hand of Eric Fenby, Boosey & Hawkes archives, pp. 20, dated.

Publication: 1931, Hawkes & Sons 6929, pp. 12, 7. 'Phrased and edited by May Harrison and Eric Fenby.' The 1973 reprint corrected the few errors in the original plates.

Performance: 6 November 1930, London, Wigmore Hall, May Harrison and Arnold Bax.

Arrangement: 'Adapted and edited for Viola' and piano by Lionel Tertis, published 1932 by Boosey & Hawkes 7215, pp. 12, 7. (Separate viola part issued with original piano score).

Notes: TB 208; EF 31–3, 91–2, 96.
Some sketches for material used in this work date from the 1920s, see Jelka Delius to Grainger, 4 November 1930, and to Ernest Newman, 28 October 1930. According to EF 91, the portions in question were:
The opening bars, a subsidiary theme and the germ of the second subject in 1;
A few bars of 2;
The themes of 3.
The central melody of 2 was Delius's first dictation to Eric Fenby, see EF 31–3.

A printed copy marked by Sir Thomas Beecham is in the DT Archive.

IX Pianoforte solos:

IX/1 ZUM CARNIVAL POLKA
Piano solo   (C maj–A min. No tempo indicated)

Date: 1885 (TB 28). See notes below also.

Dedication: 'Dedicated to Wm. Jahn, Jacksonville, Fla.'

MS: Untraced.

Publication: A. B. Campbell, Jacksonville, Fla. 'Copyright 1892 by Wm.
Jahn', pp. 5. (Copies in Library of Congress and in Jacksonville Public
Library). Title page and first page of music reproduced in GC 18–19.
Xerox copy, DT Archive. To be included in an Album of piano solos by
Delius in hand (1977) for publication by Boosey & Hawkes.

Notes: Not in PW.
TB 28 states that the work, 'a lively polka, . . . was published at the
beginning of 1885 in Jacksonville', but gives no supporting evidence for
his date. The Library of Congress copy bears the copyright date: Jan 20
1892.
I am indebted to William and Janet Randel for a private communication
in which they state: 'The first real U.S. Copyright was issued in July 1891
(the law went into effect then), and this would account for Jahn
copyrighting it at that time. . . . Whether or not Campbell's printed "Zum
Carnival" while Delius was in Florida we have *not* been able to discover.
It seems likely they did and that when copyright became available Jahn
took advantage of it'.
Of the other works of this period mentioned by Beecham, the song *Over
the mountains high* is dated 1885 on the MS; as also, apparently, are the
Pensées Mélodieuses for piano.

IX/2 **PENSÉES MÉLODIEUSES**
Piano solo

Date: 1885 (MS).

Dedication: ?

MS: Autograph listed on Beecham Libr. list in the 1950s, dated 1885.
  ?Beecham library.

Publication: none.

Notes: Not in PW.
  TB 28 states: 'there are also a few short piano pieces, among them "Zum
  Carnival"'.

IX/3 NORWEGISCHER SCHLITTENFAHRT
[Norwegian Sleigh Ride]
Piano solo

Date: 1887 (see below).

Dedication: ?

MS: Lost.

Publication: none in this original form but see p. 129 supra.

Arrangement: for orchestral version by the Composer and transcriptions thereof, see *Three Small Tone Poems*, 1890, no. 2, 'Winter Night', p. 129 supra.

Notes: PW 27 (46) refers to this as an orchestral work entitled *Schlittenfahrt* composed for the Christmas Eve party given by Grieg in 1887 for Delius, Sinding and Halvorsen but implies that Grieg's hospitality prevented the actual performance. Grieg, however, wrote (in the small hours of Christmas morning): 'Mr. Delius [played] a piano piece which he called "Norwegian Sleigh Ride" with the greatest of talent', (Grieg to Frants Beyer, '1st day of Christmas, 1887').

IX/4 BADINAGE
Piano solo.   (Giocoso, D flat major)

Date: 18. .?

Dedication: none.

MS: (*a*). In the hand of an unidentified copyist, bold and very clear, DT 35 ff 15–16 (RL 112), pp. 4, undated. Headed 'Badinage/F. Delius' in the composer's hand, probably at a later date.

(*b*). 2 pages of autograph sketches for the work, DT 39 f 63 (RL 142).

Publication: *See plates 27–28*.

Notes: Not in PW.
Despite the undoubted 'style populaire' which presupposes an early date, the careful drafts in DT 39 give the impression of a mid-1890s work.

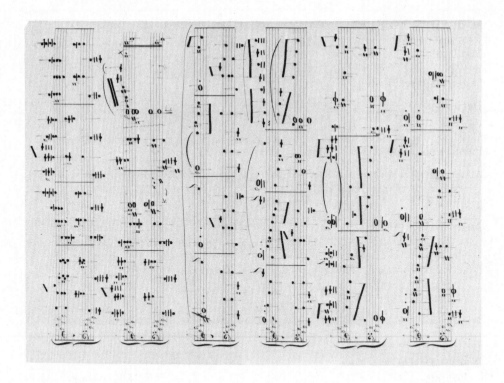

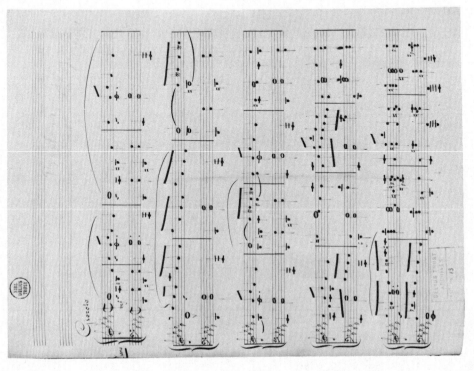

Plates 27–8: Piano piece, *Badinage* (in a copyist's hand)

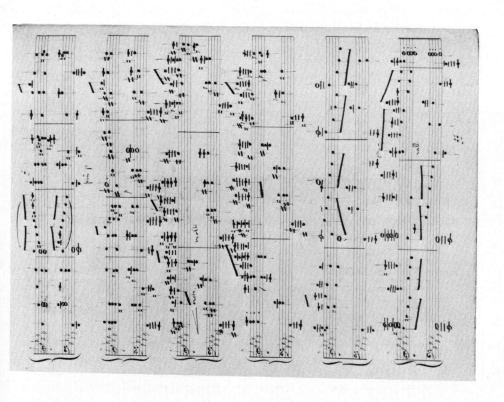

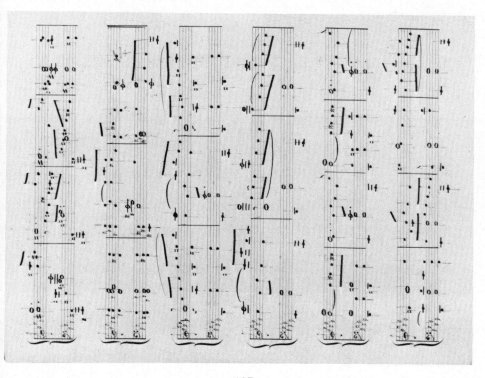

IX/5 [TWO PIANO PIECES]
[1] Valse 1890 [29 bars]
[2] [Reverie] (unfin.) [29 bars]

Date: 1889–90 (MS).

Dedication: none.

MS: (*a*). Autograph, 1 leaf, oblong, signed and dated at head *Croissy 1889–1890—Fr. Delius*, Moldenhauer Archive (photo copy, DT Archive).

(*b*). An incomplete pencil copy of 2 in Jelka Delius's hand, DT 35 ff 17b–18a (RL 113), with some differences but with the title 'Rêverie'. *See plates 29–30.*

Publication: 1, unpubl. in this version. For publication of later version of 1, see *Five Piano Pieces* 1923, no. 3.

2, orig. MS unpubl. For Jelka Delius's incomplete copy, see plate 29.

Notes: PW 160 (198).
1. Valse: bars 1–23 correspond, with some small changes, to bars 1–23 of the later version. Some alterations marked in the autograph are of interest, as the later (published) version sometimes ignores them. Bar 24 was apparently a later interpolation, bb. 24–28 being inked over pencil drafts of 25–29. The piece ends in E flat. (The later, published, version differed at bar 24 and, after 8 other new bars, returned to the opening 11 bars followed by 7 bars conclusion in the opening key of G.)
2. Jelka Delius's MS of the *Reverie* is simpler and less complete than the autograph. Even the latter, however, is incompletely realized in the last line.

IX/6 **DANCE FOR HARPSICHORD**
Tanz für Harpsichord

(A minor)

Date: 1919 (first edition).

Dedication: 'For Mrs. Violet Gordon Woodhouse'.

MS: (*a*). Autograph, BL Add. 50497, n.d. pp. 2, ink over pencil; microfilm, DT archive.

(*b*). Autograph pencil sketch, DT 39 f 89a (RL 146).

Publication: Dec 1919, *Music and Letters*, Vol. 1 no. 1 (Jan 1920), pp. [73–75], printed from type and entitled: Harpsichord piece, composed for Mrs. Gordon Woodhouse, 1919. 'With graceful dance movement, rather quick'.

1922, Universal Edition 7037, engraved, pp. 3. 'Grazioso, piùtosto un poco vivo'.

1939, Transferred to Boosey & Hawkes; later reprinted unaltered, 15167.

Notes: TB 182.

There are a few very small differences between the MS and the second (engraved) publication. In some (though not all) of these cases, the MS agrees with the *first* edition.

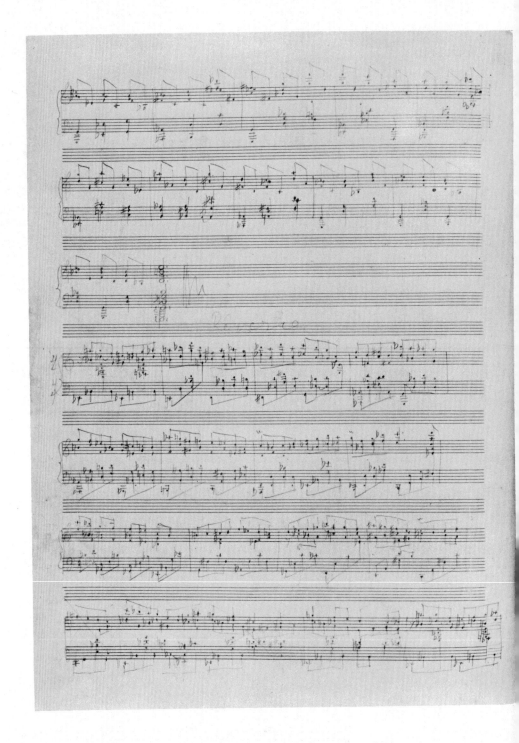

Plate 29: Piano pieces (conclusion of *Valse*; commencement of *Rêverie*) drafts in Jelka Delius's hand

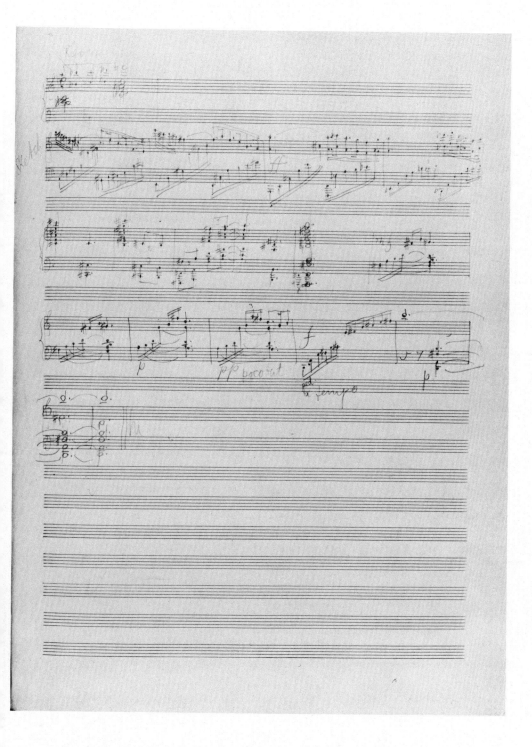

Plate 30: Piano pieces (continuation of *Rêverie*; conclusion of [*Prelude*])
drafts in Jelka Delius's hand

191

IX/7 **FIVE PIANO PIECES**
FÜNF KLAVIERSTÜCKE

1–2. Mazurka and Waltz for a Little Girl
(Mazurka und Walzer für ein kleines Mädchen)
(Con moto, F major; Lento, Tempo di Valse, C major).
3. Waltz (Gracefully and with verve, G major) 'Croissy 1891 (finished at
Grez sur Loing 1922)'.
4. Lullaby for a Modern Baby (Wiegenlied für ein modernes Baby) (Very
slow, D major).
5. Toccata (A minor)

Date: 1922–3 and see above (MS).

Dedication: 'For Evlyn Howard-Jones' in printed copies; but nos. 1 & 2
probably for Yvonne O'Neill.

MS: (*a*). Copies in Jelka Delius's hand, DT 35 ff 19–22, 17 (RL 112–4), nos.
1 (Petite Valse 1923), 2 (1923), 3 and 4 (1922) in ink; another copy of 3 in
pencil ('with grace and vigor').

(*b*). *Stichvorlagen* in Jelka Delius's hand, Universal Edition Archiv, BL
Loan 54/1, nos. 1–5, pp. 1, 1, 2, 2, 3 (microfilm, DT Archive).

(*c*). Another copy of 2 in Jelka Delius's hand, 'For Yvonne O'Neill', coll.
Mrs. Derek Hudson (Yvonne O'Neill). This is probably the 'seventh one'
referred to, see Notes to *Three Preludes* inf.

Publication: 1925, Universal Edition 7947 (different impressions; with Engl.
only, and with bilingual covers and titlepages) pp. 11—No. 4 separately,
for voice or violin and piano, Universal Edition 7929.

1939, Transferred to Boosey & Hawkes Inc. who later reprinted the work
unaltered. Originally reversing the pagination, later printings followed
the UE layout.

Arrangement: An orchestral version of these pieces, made by Eric Fenby for
the Wadham College Music Society, was performed at Oxford under D.
O. Tall on 16 May 1964. Orchestra:
1. 1. 2. 1—2. 1. 0. 0—Timp. (opt.)—Strings (solo viola in no. 4).
MS, Boosey & Hawkes archives, pp. 35. ("Five Little Pieces").

Notes: The Toccata was originally entitled *Etude* and was numbered IV, as
can be seen from MS(b). A red pencil query ?*Tempo* remained
unanswered. There are a number of very small differences between the
Stichvorlage (b) and the printed edition, not affecting the notes; also a
number of 'precautionary accidentals' were inserted (probably by UE's
reader) and the layout of b. 17 of no. 5 was garbled.

IX/8 THREE PRELUDES
Piano solo

1. Scherzando (D major)
2. Quick   (D major)
3. Con moto   (D major)

Date: 1923 (see below).

Dedication: 1, 'For Howard Jones'; 2, 'For Adine O'Neill'; (3, none).

MS: (*a*). Pencil draft of 1, headed 'Prelude III', in Jelka Delius's hand, DT 35 f 18 (RL 113), with slightly shorter ending, *see plate 30*.

(*b*). *Stichvorlage*, in Jelka Delius's hand, lost.

Publication: 1923, Anglo-French Music Co., London, 219, pp. 9.
Universal Edition 9557 (=the same?) [not seen].
Transferred to Oxford University Press, the present owners of
A.-F. M. Co., and later reprinted with a few added fingerings and
editorial markings.

Notes: In Derek Hudson's 'Norman O'Neill' (Quality Press, 1945), pp. 71–2, extracts from letters from Delius and Jelka Delius to Norman and Adine O'Neill explain the origin of all these late piano pieces. In March 1923 Jelka Delius sent MSS of 'seven little piano pieces' to Adine O'Neill, explaining that they were her 'debut as an amanuensis, as [he] cannot write and has to dictate it all to me . . .' Delius intended to compose easy pieces for his god-daughter, Yvonne O'Neill; 'they always grew too difficult, but the seventh one, we think, is quite easy.'
The programme note to the second concert of the 1929 Festival states that the other pieces were written immediately after the preludes.

I think 1922?

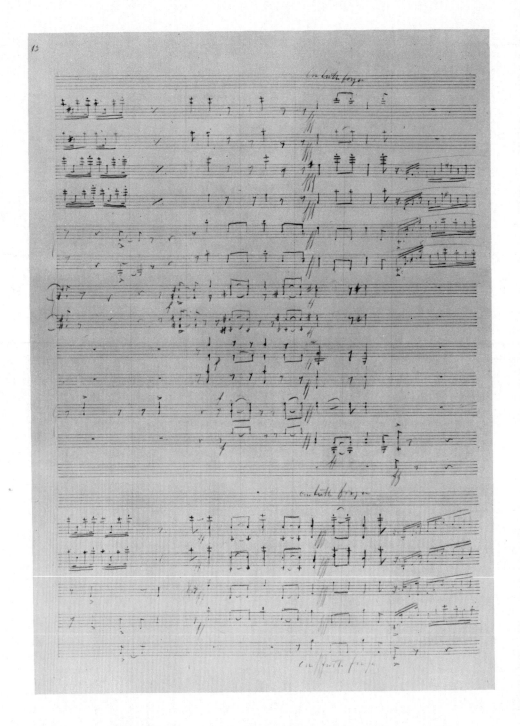

Plate 31: draft score of Grieg's op. 19 no. 2, orchestrated by Delius, page 13

X Appendix:

(i) Arrangements, collaborated works etc.

1. [Swedish folk-songs arranged by FD].

    Date: 1888.
    MS: unlocated.
    Notes: LKC 17. Leonard Labatt to FD, 2 October 1888: 'I will take with me the Swedish song for which you have done an accompaniment, and sing it in America'. Labatt wrote that he would be glad if FD would set a few more 'Swedish folk-songs arranged by FD'.

2. AUS DEM VOLKSLEBEN
    Humoresken von Edvard Grieg [op. 19] No. 2.
    Norwegischer Brautzug im Vorüberziehen.
    Orchestrirt von Fritz Delius.

    Date: '(le 2 Dec^ber 1889)'.
    Orchestra: Picc. 2. 2. 2. 2—4. 2. 2 Cornets. 3. 1—Timp.—Strings.
    MS: Autograph pencil draft score DT 3 ff 69–78 (RL 26), pp. 18, dated. Unpublished. *See plate 31.*
    Note: This piano work was earlier orchestrated by Halvorsen for inclusion in Grieg's incidental music to *Peer Gynt* as op. 23 no. 2.

3. [according to the list 1935/2].
    'Small piece composed in Jotunheim (Norway) jointly by Grieg, Sinding and Delius, MS.' [1890?]. Lost.

4. Delius et Papus [Dr. Gérard Encausse].
    'Anatomie & Physiologie de l'Orchestre.'

    Publ. Chamuel, Editeur, 29 Rue de Trévise, Paris, 1894, pp. 24.
    Notes: PW 49; LKC 34–6. Copies are to be found in Bibl. Nat. and Library of Congress.
    Properly considered a literary work, this pamphlet is included here because of its musical subject-matter.

5. The mystery of the legend 'rev. par Frédéric Delius' appearing beneath the Composers' names on Zoltán Kodály's *10 pièces pour le piano* (op. 3) and Béla Bartók's *2 Román Tanc* (op. 8a) in the editions first published in 1910 by Rózsavölgyi & Co. (3324, 3333), also found in some copies with Universal Edition covers (e.g. Bartók 6857), is satisfactorily explained by Beecham (TB 191), who also quotes an undated letter from Kodály on the subject. Delius's editorial functions were nil; the agreed use of his name as reviser was for establishment of foreign copyright purposes only. See also DLP 66.

(ii) Notebooks, sketches etc.

1. *Notebook I.*   MS: Jacksonville University.

   Containing chiefly the early exercises in harmony and counterpoint
   carried out under Thomas Ward's instruction at Solana Grove, Florida,
   in 1884. Also, and presumably from a slightly later date, are drafts for the
   early unaccompanied part-songs *Oh! Sonnenschein*, *Ave Maria* and
   Sonnenscheinlied. Fair copies of these are now in DT 36, see separate
   entry for *Six part-songs with German texts*. The first draft setting of
   Sonnenscheinlied differs musically from the definitive one. A facsimile of
   a page of this notebook is reproduced in DLP p. 13.

2. *Notebook II.*   MS: Grainger Museum, Melbourne, Australia.

   Containing some exercises similar to those in notebook I above, followed
   by sketches for 4-part chorus, including two draft settings of *Frühlingsanbruch* (fair copy now in DT 36, as above). Here also, the first setting is
   entirely different from the definitive one. This notebook was apparently
   used for a longer period; a series of instrumental pieces—sketched under
   the heading *Skizzenbuch—Fritz Delius* probably date from the early
   Leipzig days; and miscellaneous sketches, some headed *Rhapsody*, are of
   an even later date. See also SM7, 74.

3. *Notebook III*   MS: DT 38 ff 1–42 (RL 133)

   Containing first a series of *Norske Wiser* dated *Norway, July 18th 87* and
   other dates the same month. Also, dated *August 5th* a setting in an earlier
   version (Ger. words) of the Ibsen 'Cradle Song' ('Little Håkon') (for
   published version, see 7 Songs from the Norwegian, no. 1, p. 95 above).
   An orchestral piece dated *Aug. 1889, Leirungs Hytte, Jotunheim, Norge*,
   but incomplete, also occurs.
   Draft pages headed *Hiawatha* and *Feast at Solhaug* are to be identified;
   also, under the heading *Vorspiel*, a sketch for part of the prelude to Act
   III of *Irmelin* (1892), though not so entitled. A short-score sketch of the
   principal section of the last movement of *Florida* (1887) can also be
   recognized.

4. 'Larger small sketch book' (to use Grainger's Red Indian-like
   terminology).   MS: Grainger Museum.

   Sketches for works of the period 1914–17, e.g. the Cello Sonata, String
   Quartet, Violin Concerto, Two unaccompanied choruses and Requiem
   are to be found in this most interesting volume; as well as the first draft
   of a song to Yeats' words 'The Lake Isle of Innisfree' and some pages so
   far still unidentified, probably dating from the early 1920s.
   See also SM7, 74–6.

5. 'Smaller small sketch book'.   MS: Grainger Museum.

   Principally, this little book contains the first two-stave draft for *The Song
   of the High Hills*. Various other material, some resembling part of
   Fennimore and Gerda, continues up to the early 1920s. See also SM7, 76.

6. A large number of miscellaneous sketch-sheets, drafts etc., covering
   the whole of Delius's working life, were gathered together, placed in
   order and bound into DT 39 ff 1–115 by Rachel Lowe, and were
   described in considerable detail by her in RL 134–149. Reference has
   already been made to certain individual items therein; but the whole

Konvolut is a fascinating and most valuable contribution to the study of FD's methods of working. Eric Fenby recalls that voluminous sketches, preliminaries to Delius's almost entire *œuvre*, formerly existed at Grez; the bulk of these were apparently destroyed by Jelka shortly after Delius's death. The value of the few surviving items listed above, especially those now forming DT 39, is thus enhanced.

(iii) A Conspectus of Delius's principal compositions

set out in categories, and in their approximate chronological positions (with some performance notes in the case of the dramatic works).

	Dramatic works	Voices & orch.	Solo voice & orch.	Songs, choruses
1884				
5				Early songs
6				
7				Early unacc. choruses
8	*Zanoni* project; other abortive		*Paa Vidderne* (melodrama)	5 Songs from the Norwegian
9	projects, *Emperor & Galilean* etc.,		*Sakuntala*	7 Songs from the Norwegian
1890	crystallizing to:			
1			*Maud*	Shelley songs
2	*Irmelin*			
3				Various songs
4	*The Magic Fountain*			
5				Verlaine songs
6				
7	*Koanga* *Folkeraadet*		*Seven Danish Songs*	
8	first libretto of *V. R. & J.*	*Mitternachtslied Zarathustras*		*Nietzschelieder*
9	Parts of *Koanga* perf. in concert			
1900	*A Village*			Danish songs
1	*Romeo and Juliet*			'Black Roses'
2	*Margot la Rouge*	*Appalachia*		'Summer Landscape'
3	*Salomé* project	*Sea Drift*		
4	*Koanga* perf.			
5		*A Mass of Life* (incorporating		
6		*Mitternachtslied Zarathustras*)		
7	*V. R. & J.* perf in Berlin	*Songs of Sunset*	*Cynara* sketched	*On Craig Ddu* & other unacc.
8				choruses
9	*Fennimore & Gerda*			

	Orchestral	Solo instr. & orch.	Chamber music	Piano solo etc.
1884				
5				*Zum Carnival*
				Pensées
6				*Mélodieuses*
	Florida			
7				*Norwegian*
				Sleigh Ride
8	*Hiawatha*	*Suite* for violin	String quartet	
	Marche Caprice	& orch		
9	(*Florida* revised)		*Romance* for violin	
				Two piano pieces
1890	3 small tone	*Légendes* (Sagen)		
	poems	for PF & orch.		
1	*Paa Vidderne*			
2			Sonata in B for	
			violin & piano	
3			String quartet?	
4		*Légende* in E flat		
		for Vl. & orch.		
5	*Over the Hills*			
	and far away.			
6	*Appalachia*		*Romance* for cello	
7		Piano Concerto		
		in C minor		
8	*La Ronde se*			
	déroule			
9				
	Paris			
1900				
1	*Life's Dance*			
2				
3				
4				
5			Sonata (no. 1)	
			for violin sketched	
6				
7	*Brigg Fair*			
8	*In a Summer Garden*			
	A Dance Rhapsody			
9				

	Dramatic works	Voices & orch.	Solo voice & orch.	Songs, choruses Miscell. songs.
1910	V. R. & J. perf. in London			
1		The Song of the High Hills		
2		Arabesk		
3				
4	Plans to produce Fennimore in Cologne			
5		Requiem		
6				Old English Lyrics
7	other plans: (Wuthering Heights,			'To be sung of a summer night on the water'
8	Deirdre of the Sorrows)			(unacc. chorus)
9	Fennimore perf. in Frankfurt			
1920	Hassan commission			
1				
2				
3	Hassan perf.			
4				'The Splendour falls' (unacc. chorus)
5			'A Late Lark'	
6				
7				
8				
9			Cynara completed	
1930		Songs of Farewell		
1				
2		Idyll		
3				
4				

	Orchestral	Solo instr. & orch.	Chamber music	Piano solo etc.
1910				
1	Two pieces for small orchestra			
2				
3				
4	North Country Sketches		Violin Sonata no. 1 finished	
5	Air and Dance			
6	A Dance Rhapsody (no. 2)	Double Concerto Violin Concerto	Cello Sonata String Quartet	
7	Eventyr			
8	A Song before Sunrise			
9	Poem of Life & Love			Dance for Harpsichord
1920		Cello Concerto		
1				
2				
3			Violin Sonata no. 2	Five piano pieces Three preludes
4				
5				
6				
7				
8				
9				
1930	A Song of Summer Irmelin prelude	Caprice & Elegy (Cello & orch.)	Violin Sonata no. 3	
1				
2	Fantastic Dance			
3				
4				

Notes

Index